Usui Reiki

Level One Training Manual

A Manual for Instructors
and a Workbook for Students

Francine Milford
Reiki Master/Teacher

Usui Reiki
by Francine Milford

Copyright 2003

Online editions may also be available for this title. For more information, please visit us at www.lulu.com.

Lulu Enterprises, Inc.

ISBN: 1-4116-0074-6

Table of Contents

Disclaimer

The information given in this book is not meant to diagnose or give recommendations and advice about the treatment of any illness. If you are ill, consult your physician or primary health care practitioner before pursuing any form of therapy on your own. This author makes no claims or guarantees to your healing or self-transformation.

Francine Milford

Usui Reiki Level One

-a Training Manual for Instructors

and a Workbook for Students

Illustrations by Larry, Paul and Francine Milford

ISBN   1-4116-0074-6

Printed in the United States of America

This book is dedicated
to all the Reiki Masters
who have gone before me

Foreword

Within the pages of this book are the beginnings of a spiritual awakening. Francine Milford, a holistic practitioner and Reiki Master, has put her teaching style and information into this instructional manual geared towards other Reiki Masters to use as a workbook for their own students in their classes.

For students wanting to learn the basics, up to seasoned Reiki master practitioners, this book will offer everyone a new and fresh perspective on the Reiki system of natural healing. Francine offers her own view point on many of the long held beliefs of Reiki masters. It is also Francine's belief that Reiki does not need to be complicated or run by a set of rules that are carved in stone. As energy, Reiki must be left to flow freely through the practitioner in a way that is unique between the practitioner, the client, and the energy itself.

The beauty of the Reiki system of natural healing lies in its simplicity. So simple that even children can give Reiki treatments. So simple, that even pets can be attuned to Reiki and give their owners a Reiki treatment with the touch of a paw. Throughout this book, Francine exudes a love for Reiki and all of its applications in day to day living. She also dispels some of the myths that have shrouded Reiki in secrecy. Reiki is no longer a secret shared only by master and student, it is now open to the public to view and ponder over.

This book will give you a wonderful insight into the many processes associated with Reiki. You will find compelling evidence of how Reiki can work in your own life, as well as for those you love and care for. Francine brings her years of experience as a Reiki Master and healer into the methods and techniques of the Reiki system of natural healing. Through her extensive experience as an alternative practitioner, she adds insights to some of the most general basic principles of natural healing.

Acknowledgments

This book has been several years in the creation process. When I started teaching Reiki eight years ago, I used the manuals and coursework that had been handed down to me by my Reiki Master. As I continued learning and receiving information from other Reiki Masters and from my own observations, I began to change and adapt the information that I included in my own Reiki manuals. Soon I discovered that the Reiki manuals I gave to my own students were truly my own. It is this compilation of information that has been in the process of creating this book and it is to these wonderful sources of energy that I would like to express my gratitude.

I have been blessed with many wonderful teachers, guides and family support. If it were not for this help and support, I may still be in the creating and waiting stages and not moving forward.

Special recognition is due to Merle Sunde', an R.N. and Light worker who created the video, Reiki. This beautifully created tape has been seen by hundreds of my own students. I thank her for her wonderful portrayal in the video and for the information she shares. She is has been an inspiration.

I would also like to thank my own wonderful Reiki Masters from all my separate and unique Reiki lineages. I honor them and their gift to me. You can view some of them in the lineage section towards the back of the book.

Most importantly, I want to thank my children who had to pose for most of the pictures in this book. It wasn't easy for them, but they have blessed me beyond measure in being there for me and permitting me to use their pictures in the book, and on the Internet. Thank you, Larry and Paul.

And to my students who encouraged me to create this book. They gave me the incentive to keep at it and encouraged me not to let this idea fall by the wayside. It has been a path of self discovery and personal transformation. Thank you to all my students.

Lastly and most importantly, thank you to my husband. Although he does not believe in Reiki in the same way that I do, he is more of a blessing than he realizes. Being a scientist at heart, he sees the world in the physical sense and has allowed me to bounce many an idea and method off of him. He is able to explain in scientific words, why something would work, or not. I love that and I love him. His scientific mind helps me to better describe to others the intricacies of energy work.

Thank You All

Introduction

Today, there is a need for healing that goes beyond just the physical body. The need runs deep into the mental and emotional soul of the human spirit. People are searching for answers for illnesses in their life. They are looking for a way to become whole again.

There are many paths to wholeness, many systems of healing. Some people choose to go to conventional doctors and listen to conventional wisdom. Other people choose to go to Alternative practitioners and begin a journey of self discovery and understanding. I, myself, began this journey many years ago through my own physical problems.

I was around 39 years old when I started to get severe and debilitating migraines. I would literally go blind during an attack. This was especially frightening to me since I was the mother of a 4 year old and part of a car pool. How could I be responsible for all those little lives with me behind the wheel? How would I handle an attack while I was transporting these little children? There were no answers and then things began to get worse. Then came the panic attacks.

For those who don't know what a panic attack is, or who think it is trivial, take it from me, it is not. Since I was unfamiliar with what it was, it feels like a heart attack. In fact, it was so horrible to me that I actually had my first out of body experience during an attack. Back then, I was unfamiliar with alternative anything, so I went to the doctors for help. I was given a prescription and went home and tried 1 pill. Let me tell you the experience of taking just that 1 pill. That 1 pill took over my body so completely that I had to lie on the couch because I couldn't stand. Once on the couch, I couldn't lift my head up from the couch. I was extremely frightened but the drug made be not care. It was weird, laying there knowing that if the house caught on fire, I could not get up and save myself or my child who was playing on the floor next me, and I wouldn't care. This was also the same day I saw my first aura. Well, at least that was pretty cool.

It was a good thing that my husband was home that day and we just had to wait out the effects of the drug which took about 6 hours to wear off so that I could stand again. I reported this to the doctor who calmly answered me, "Oh, just take 1/2 the dose next time." Next time? Oh, I had decided there wasn't going to be a next time. I wanted to return to my old health self and I had to find a different way to get that accomplished.

This is where I began looking into alternative healing. The first book I ever read to begin my journey was the Celestine Prophecy by James Redfield. This book alone opened doors and avenues that I never felt possible. I learned what an aura was. I had seen auras since I was a child and went to the eye doctor because I thought something was wrong with my eyes. He couldn't find anything wrong with my eyes and didn't know how to explain what it was that I saw. Now I do. I then joined a discussion group at the local bookstore that had been formed to discuss the Celestine Prophecy. It was totally wonderful. It was here that I met people who introduced me to the world of alternative healing.

We ended up moving within months and I had to leave my curiosity behind. However, once we were settled in our move: Venice, Florida, other doors began to open. I joined a group who was discussing Louise Hays book, "You Can Heal your Life". Well, that was it. I questioned that poor instructor over and over again. There was so much I wanted to learn and know. I was a sponge and this was only the beginning. We become great friends - thank you Shelby!

It was at this time that I began taking courses in Herbology, Aromatherapy, Bach Flower, and more. I was also a Fitness Specialist and started to learn Qigong. Qigong is a very, very powerful form of martial arts and should not be used and practiced by just anyone. It was through the practice of Qigong that I became familiar with working with energy. Wanting to work in an energy system that would be safe to use on children, I began to pray. I wanted a system that worked on unconditional love and acceptance. A giving and loving system, not one based on fear. The next day there was an ad for a Reiki Level One training class about an hour or so drive from my home. In the ad it stated, "A safe and loving energy". That was it, my prayers had been answered and I called and signed up. The rest is history.

I finished my Reiki Level One training in a two day workshop and went back a month later for my Reiki Level II training. Some time passed before I found a Reiki Master and finished my training. After several years of teaching Reiki and using the information that was handed down by my master, I began to take additional Reiki training from other Reiki Masters. I explored new methods and techniques, compared symbols and their uses, and even tried new attunement processes. I have incorporated the best of ALL of my teachings into my own personal manuals.

Reiki has literally changed my life. I am not the same person who stumbled into the first class not even knowing what a "Chakra" was. I felt foolish and naive then, but somehow I knew that I was meant to be here and that I was meant to learn Reiki - the Universe was right.

This book is my way of thanking all my students who have blessed me with their presence in my Reiki classes both in person and through the Internet. I offer you my sincerest and deepest gratitude for allowing me the opportunity and privilege of sharing Reiki attunements with you.

You have all confirmed the truth that we are all one in the Universal consciousness. That we share all that was past, is present, and will be in the future. We are all connected. We are all one.

When you use your gift of Reiki, you honor me and all those who have gone before me. And most importantly, when we use our gift of Reiki, we honor ourselves and everything on this planet. So use your gift, often.

"May Light and Love Surround You Always"

Francine Milford

"Come to the edge, he said.
They said: We are afraid.
Come to the edge, he said.
They came, he pushed
them...
and they flew. "

- Guillaume Appolinaire

Chapter One

History of Reiki

What is Reiki?

Reiki, (pronounced ray-key), in the Japanese Character system, is a combination of two separate words. "Rei" meaning "universal, spirit, a boundless essence" and "Ki" meaning "life force energy". Together their meaning is roughly "Universal Life Energy", or "Universal Life Force Energy".

Life force energy resides in everything you see around you, yourself included. All animals, plants, humans, have life force energy. The ancient discipline of Qigong is the practice of gathering up this energy and directing it into parts, or areas, of the body. When a person dies, this life force energy departs the body. For you to understand and experience this life force energy, I have devised some simple exercises for you to perform.

Exercise 1:

As an exercise to feel this energy, begin by rubbing your hands briskly together for one minute. Bring your mind's focus to your hands. Now, slowly and gently, pull your hands apart about 1-3" from each other. Slowly bring your hands in together, without touching, and take them apart a few inches. Do this for a few minutes to feel the energy. That is your life force energy. Write in the space below your experiences and any sensations you had while doing this exercise:

_____

_____

_____

_____

_____

_____

_____

_____

_____

_____

_____

Exercise 2:

You will need a partner or volunteer for this exercise.

Rub your hands briskly together again as you did the above exercise. Bring the focus of your mind to your hands. Have your partner or volunteer do the same thing. This time, bring your hands to 1-3" from your partners hands. Slowly bring the hands together without touching and then bring them 1-3" apart. Do this a few times and write down below any sensations you experienced with this exercise:

_____

_____

_____

_____

_____

_____

Write down here any sensations that your partner or volunteer experienced with this exercise:

_____

_____

_____

_____

_____

_____

Now, try the exercise again, but this time place your hands on different parts of your partner or volunteer's body (such as their thigh, knee, elbow, or shoulder). Be sure their eyes are closed and see if they can identify where your hand is. After a few times, trade places and see if you can locate their hand on your body. Write down your discoveries here:

_____

_____

_____

_____

_____

_____

_____

_____

_____

_____

_____

_____

Exercise 3:

In this exercise, you will experience seeing your aura, the life force energy that surrounds all living things. To do this you will rub your hands briskly together once again. Focus your mind on your hands. Now place your hands, palms facing you above your head. Have the fingers of both hands facing each other and keep them about 1/2 inches apart. It is also helpful if the ceiling behind your hands is white. Now, allow your eyes to go out of focus and just lazily stare at the space between the tips of your middle fingers. In time, you will be able to see a haze appear around your fingers. This haze will be translucent or opal in appearance. This is your life force energy. With practice, you will also begin to see a second layer form. This layer has a jagged edge and is blue in color. This is a layer of your aura. Write down your experiences with this exercise. Do not be too hard on yourself if you did not see anything while trying this exercise. With patience and practice you will succeed:

_____

_____

_____

_____

_____

_____

_____

_____

When working with Reiki energies we can significantly alter and modify the layers of energy that surround each and every one of us. Reiki works on ALL levels for healing, both inside our bodies dealing with physical, emotional and mental healing, as well as, outside of our bodies dealing with the many layers of our aura (our first defense against disease and illness).

Exercise 4:

To help you experience the possibilities of working with the energy, I want you to do the following exercise: Rub your hands briskly together again. Bring your mind's focus to your hands. Take your hands and place them, palms facing each other in front of you. I want you to play with this energy by pulling your hands apart and bringing them together. You can play with expanding the energy in front you. Make the energy between your hands larger and larger each time you come together and pull apart. You can also compress this energy into an egg shape of concentrated energy and place this egg of energy into a particular body area, or organ. It is very helpful in your Reiki practice, to become familiar and learn to work with energy. It is NOT necessary to become an energy expert in order to practice Reiki; it is just one more tool you can place in your little black bag of healing systems. Write down any sensations or experiences you had while doing this exercise:

_____

_____

_____

_____

_____

_____

Reiki is a safe, natural, and holistic way of treating yourselves and others who are suffering from many acute and chronic conditions. It helps to bring about physical, mental, spiritual, and emotional well being. Conditions that Reiki may improve include stress, menstrual problems, pain, insomnia, anxiety, tension, headaches, asthma, anxiety attacks, and intestinal gas.

Reiki is not a substitute for traditional medicine. No Reiki practitioner should ever tell a client that they can "cure" an illness or advise their client to stop taking any prescribed medicines or to stop seeing their doctor. This is very bad business, and the Reiki practitioner must stay out of the choices their client's are making. It is both unethical and illegal to make suggestions such as these to any client.

The History of Reiki

As the story goes.......Dr. Mikao Usui, a 19 Century Christian Monk was teaching his class one day when a student asked the question, "Show us the methods that Jesus used to heal the blind and walk on water". Usui answered that he did not know how to do these things but had faith that Jesus did indeed accomplish these and other feats of healing. His students replied, "We do not want to live on faith, but we want to see with our own eyes". This prompted the good doctor to find the answers that he himself had been asking. Usui believed there was a system of healing out there in the world and He began his journey to find that system.

Usui's journey led him to America where he attended the University of Chicago and became a Doctor of Theology. He still had not found the answers that he was seeking in Christian writings regarding hands-on healing so he traveled to North India. He studied the Holy Writings while he stayed there. He still received no answers. He then returned to Japan where he started to translate Sanskrit Buddhist Sutras where he found formulas and symbols. Having found the symbols, he needed a way to activate them.

Usui decided to perform a 21 day fast at the Holy Mountain of Kuriyama. He set out 21 stones in front of him. Each day he would cast out one stone. On the 21st and last day of his fast and meditation, he saw a shining light coming towards him at great speed. It struck him in the Ajna center (middle of the forehead) and knocked him unconscious. He saw millions of little colored bubbles that contained symbols in them. Along with the lights, came the knowledge of how to activate them. He had found what he was searching for.

In ancient tradition, proof of receiving information from meditation was expected to be proven by the occurrence of three miracles. According to the Reiki story, the following are the three miracles that occurred following Usui's meditation.

(1) When Usui returned to his natural waking state of consciousness, he was elated and began to run down the mountain. Being in a weakened state from fasting, he stumbled, fell, and his toe was bleeding. He instantly grabbed his toe in both of his hands and both the bleeding and the pain stopped. This was the first miracle.

(2) He was hungry and stopped at a wayside inn where the innkeeper told Usui not to eat such a large meal after a fast, but Usui ate and was not sick. This was the second miracle.

(3) The innkeeper's daughter was in great pain from a bad toothache for many days. Usui laid his hands upon her swollen face and she immediately

felt better. This was the Third miracle.

Upon Usui's return to his monastery he decided to go into the slums of Kyoto to treat the beggars and help them to live a better life. He worked for seven years in an asylum treating many illnesses. One day he noticed some of the same people returning for treatments. When he asked them why they had not begun to live their new lives, he was told that working for a living was too hard, they preferred to beg. Usui was deeply saddened by this and wept. He realized that he had forgotten the most important ingredient in his healing work, "gratitude". Usui then wrote the following principles:

Ethical Principles of Reiki:

The Secret Method of Inviting Blessings

The Spiritual Medicine of Many Illnesses

For Today only, do not Worry, Do Not Anger

Do Your Work with Appreciation

Be Kind to all People

Show Gratitude to Every Living Thing

Say this in the morning and at night, with hands held in prayer,

Think this in your mind; chant this with your mouth.

By Dr. Mikao Usui

Principle #1

Just for Today, I will not Worry

When we spend too much time dwelling on situations and second guessing the decisions that we have made, we are doing what is called "Worrying". When we worry, we forget that there is a divine and universal design in our lives at work. In worrying, our ego believes that every outcome is directly related to what we do or don't do. This is simply not true.

In life, we are all faced with decisions that we must make. We are all faced with basic decisions such as where to live, how to make a living, and even where to buy our groceries. We make our decisions based on all previous knowledge of such things, as well as, the advice from television, newspapers, and others around us. We try to make the wisest choicest for our lives and that is all that we can do.

For some though, even if they felt they have made the best decisions for their lives, they sit at home and begin to fret and worry. "What if this happens", or "Should I have chosen the red one?" and these questions go on and on. There are no answers to these questions. All the "what ifs" and "should I have" are all counter productive and physically destroying.

You can't even worry about the future. Your worry does not add one more hour to your life, but it can take away an hour from your living. To worry about something that "may" happen in the future is also a lesson in futility. Even if the worse case scenario happened, it still would be only a lesson that the universe is giving you. All life is a lesson to be learned.

I remember a particular situation with my children. One day we were at a playground and there was another child there playing on the swings. My son wanted to play, but was unsure of how to approach the other child. "Well, what is the worse thing that could happen if you went over and said hello to the little boy playing on the swing?" I asked. My son replied, "Well, he could tell me to get lost", or "He could tell me to leave him alone". And I said, "Yes, that is all true, but now tell me, what could be the best thing that could happen?" After pondering the question for a while, he came up with, "Well, he could want to play with me and let me play with his really cool toys and we could have a really good time". So then I looked at him and said, "Well, that is also all true. So, if you already know what the worse thing that could happen is and you already know what the best thing that could happen is, you must decide if it is worth it to go over and say hello to the little boy?" And for those of you, who are waiting to hear what my son decided to do, he decided to go over and say hello to the little boy and they both had a great afternoon playing together.

I have used this scenario with adults as well. It works wonderfully to put things in perspective. When buying an automobile, jot down the pros and the cons. Then go through the scenario in your head. "What is the worst case scenario?" "What is the best case scenario?" I always weigh my decisions on this little bit of logic. Of course, you may have your own way to bring logic back into your life. With logic, one can dismiss the uncertainty that comes with worry. Some people have a scientific bent to their lives and need to have everything written out for them in black and white to make a decision that is "logical" and then they learn to accept that decision and release it. Releasing a decision that has been made takes away the ability of worry to take hold of you and second guess your decisions.

I watch as my friend buys a new blouse. First she frets over the style and the price, then over the color and the length and the fit. "What will she wear with this new blouse?" The questioning seems endless, "should I", "could I", "what if I", and on and on it goes. Then finally a purchase is made and on the way home I hear, "Oh, maybe I should have purchased the white one", or I hear, "Maybe I should have waited until it went on sale". I have to laugh. You probably have done the same thing yourself. When I catch myself second guessing a purchase, I firmly say to myself, "No, this is what I chosen for myself and I will be happy with it". Try it with determination and see if it works for you.

Assignment

In the space below, I want you to write down all the things that you are currently worrying about; this can include people, places, and situations:

_____

_____

_____

_____

_____

_____

_____

_____

_____

Of the things that you have written above, what can you do right now that will help you to stop worrying about these things?

_____

_____

_____

_____

_____

_____

_____

Starting tomorrow morning, you will wake up and for the whole day you will not worry about any single thing. If you catch yourself beginning to worry about something, stop. Just tell yourself that Just for Today, I will not worry. Write here how it feels not to worry for one whole day:

_____

_____

_____

_____

_____

_____

_____

_____

Principle #2

Just for Today, I will not Anger

Anger is one of the most dangerous and fiercest of emotions you can express. Anger can stem from feelings of guilt, shame and repressed resentments. In essence, anger is a loss of control and a desire to control. I have seen anger destroy people's self esteem, relationships, and health.

The emotion called anger settles in the heart. I have seen many people who are angry manifest physical problems with their heart. These heart problems can range from restricted blood flow in the valves of the heart to heart attacks. You see heart patients go in for heart transplants and walk out of the hospital only to return again in a few years with the same problem. Doctors know how to deal with the proper diet of the heart patient, but rarely discuss the emotions that can affect the heart.

For those people who always feel a need to control the people and situations in their life, anger can become a prison sentence. The very people and situations they want to control they end up losing because of their hot tempers and displays of anger.

When we see angry people, we like to run away from them. Some people like to stand up to these seemly bullies and fighting can begin. When we sit back and observe our own reactions to these situations, we learn something about ourselves.

Some people choose to "bite their tongue" and seethe and simmer inside. This is not good nor is it healthy. While vocal outbursts are not desirable, holding your emotions and bottling them up deep inside is not good or healthy either. You must learn how to control the emotion of anger and yet say your peace to those around you. You must learn how to stand up for what you believe to be right and just and stay strong in that conviction without the use of bodily force.

When you become more sensitive to the energies around you, you will find that the energy of anger is very disconcerting to your energy system. You may pick up the vibration of anger as thick, dark and black or smoky. It feels very heavy and very concentrated to me. When using Reiki on anger, I try to dissipate it. That is, I try to infuse the anger with the energy of Love and spread out the particles of the anger energy. The further I can spread out the particles, the weaker the anger energy becomes and the easier it is to infuse the loving and healing energy of Reiki into the client's body.

Another technique you can use to help relieve the body of excess anger build up is to "blow" the energy away. When I feel the denseness of the anger energy, I just gently blow the energy off the body. You may wish to repeat this process more than one time to accomplish this task but it is well worth it. After I blow the energy away, I begin to send Reiki energy into that area to fill it up and heal it.

Assignment

Are there people or situations that have made you angry? If so, write them down here. How did feeling the emotion of anger make you feel? What happened in your body and in your mind while you were angry?

_____

_____

_____

_____

_____

_____

On thinking back on a particular situation in which you were angry, was there a different way in which you could have reacted? And if so, how was it different?

_____

_____

_____

_____

_____

_____

Watch someone who is displaying anger. Write down below how you are feeling during this interaction. Watch the person who is angry. Look at their body language and positioning. Is their face turning red? Is their vein popping out in the neck? Are their eyes bulging? Write down your observations here:

_____

_____

_____

_____

_____

_____

_____

_____

Right now, pretend that you are angry at someone or some thing. Be aware of how your body reacts to the thought of anger. How does your mind feel when you think of the emotion of anger? Write down all your feelings and experiences here:

_____

_____

_____

_____

_____

_____

_____

_____

Now, release those feelings of anger. How does your body react to the releasing of anger from it? Is your body in a more relaxed and peaceful state? Describe your observations and sensations below:

_____

_____

_____

_____

_____

_____

_____

_____

_____

_____

Principle #3

Just for Today, I will do my work with Honor

Honesty in business is a word you don't hear about anymore. In fact, having business dealings with some corporations can be downright frustrating and dishonest. You are always placed on guard to find out if you are being lied to or taken advantage of. Dishonesty has found its way into every business, office and home.

For a Reiki practitioner though, you should strive to rise above that. One of the best traits that my employers have said of me is that I can be trusted. I have always strived to be trustworthy and honest. I would not even take a pen that did not belong to me. To me, that is not who I am striving to be. If you contemplate the cost of a pen, or an illegal IRS deduction, against the health and well being of your soul, what price are you putting on your spirit? To me, there is nothing out there in the material world that is worth having at the cost of my spirit.

When you strive to live honesty and work honesty, you are aligning yourself with the true nature of your spirit. You are divine. When you live honestly, you see the world through eyes that are clear and focused. When you work honestly, you bring honor to yourself and your family. Do not be jealous of those above you who would cheat and lie to get ahead. Do not envy them and do not copy them. You do not want to be lumped together into a group like that. You are on a spiritual path now, one following your own Divine purpose. Do not waiver.

When you are honest and truthful with yourself, you will find that you are also more honest and truthful with those around you. You will see that you do not need to build walls to keep others away from you. The more honest you are with yourself, the more honestly you see the people in your life for whom and what they are, lessons.

Assignment

Think of your own home and work ethics. How are you honest in your dealings with yourself and with others? How are you dishonest?

_____

_____

_____

_____

_____

_____

_____

_____

_____

_____

Principle #4

Just for Today, I will be Kind to All People

While it should come easily to us, many of us find it difficult to be kind to all people, at all times. Some people can really try your patience or "push your buttons". Sometimes, you can feel more generous and more tolerate but there are times when you have reached the end of the line. This happens to all of us. What is most important here is that we are trying to be more loving to the people that come into our lives.

How can you be kind to people? There are many ways in which you can accomplish this task. A smile is one of them, a kind and encouraging word is another way. When was the last time you complimented someone on something they wore? Was it an honest comment or did you have some snide and critical remark following it? When was the last time you smiled at a total stranger? It is a lot easier to return a smile than to instigate one.

When was the last time you allowed someone to push ahead of you in line without mouthing off at them? When was the last time you allowed someone to steal the fruit off your tree or cut a flower out of your garden?

When was the last time you said an encouraging word to a child and meant it? When was the last time you thanked someone for a job well done? When was the last time you went to an employer to praise an employee who had helped you find an item in the store? When was the last time you left a bigger than usual tip because a waitress went out of her way to make your meal just the way you wanted it?

If you can't think of a time when you were kind, encouraging or appreciative, then I suggest you spend some time in soul searching. Believe me, it isn't that the people around don't deserve your love and praise, they do. You must find what it is inside of you that deny you clarity in this matter. This is a serious problem and you need to work on this issue before you begin to set up a Reiki practice and work on others. Remember the old adage, "Healer, heal thyself".

Assignment

Think back on your day so far. What words of love or encouragement did you speak today? Write those words here below:

_____

_____

_____

_____

_____

_____

_____

_____

_____

_____

Principle #5

Just for Today, I will show gratitude to every living thing

Oh, this one is definitely one of my favorite. We think that we are separate from all the other things that are around us because we are human. Somehow, you are better than the trees and the plants and the rocks. For some people, they feel they are superior because they have a soul. Well, I have news for you; everything is connected in the one consciousness of the Divine.

What does this mean? This means that all the things that we see, hear, taste, eat, feel, and smell are all energy that stems from the same source, the Divine. Whatever we want to call that Source, whether we call it God or Goddess, it is the same Source for all.

Everything is alive and vibrating. It is the speed of the vibration that determines what an object is. The slower the rate of speed that an object vibrates at, the denser it becomes. Rocks vibrate at a slower rate of speed than the human body does.

When we accept and appreciate all the things that share the world with us, we are accepting and appreciating our own true selves. We are not separate from, but rather one with, all that is. All things are mirrors of our own true reflection. If we see nothing but ugliness around us, then this ugliness is but a mirror to our own inner selves. If we see nothing but beauty around us, then this beauty is a mirror of our own inner soul.

In addition, we must also learn to be grateful for those events that happen in our lives that aren't so pleasant for us. Events such as a loss of a loved one, divorce, losing a job, being robbed, losing your home to a fire, and so many other situations that leave us feeling ungrateful. How can we be grateful for these things happening in our lives? It is most difficult to find the silver lining in these dark clouds that happen in everyone's lives. These events are meant to strengthen us and give us information about ourselves in the deepest being of who we truly are. How many times have you witnessed someone you love overcome what appeared to be insurmountable odds in their lives only to come out on top stronger and healthier than ever before? Do you know someone who was told that they could never walk again and yet one year later was walking? We all have stories to share of personal triumph, of learning to reach deep within ourselves to find that strength that we never knew existed before. We all come out of the fire better than before. Our "loss" becomes our "gain".

Assignment

Right now, without thinking too much on it, what is it that you see around you? Do you see beauty, fear, sadness, joy, love, hope, possibilities....Write down here as many things as you can think of and then sit back and read them again to yourself. What pattern do you see forming?

How is the world around you reflecting your own inner self?

_____

_____

_____

_____

_____

_____

_____

_____

_____

_____

_____

Soon afterward, Dr. Mikao Usui left the asylum and returned to Kyoto. He is said to have taken a large torch and lit it. He stood with his torch in the streets of Kyoto. When someone would ask him why he was standing there with his torch, he was said to have replied," I am looking for people in search of the True Light - people who are ill and oppressed and long to be healed". This was the beginning of his healing journey as he traveled around Japan healing and teaching Reiki to others.

It is said that Usui initiated 13 men into Reiki Masterhood before his death. Usui is buried in a Kyoto temple with the story of his life written on his gravestone. It is said that his grave was honored by the Emperor of Japan, whom Usui had helped with an illness. One of Usui's students was, Chijiro Hayashi. After his Reiki Master initiation, Mr. Hayashi opened a Reiki healing Clinic in Japan. One of Mr. Hayashi's patients was a Hawayo Takata from Hawaii. She was healed of her severe illness in his clinic and wanted to learn the Reiki system of healing. After she learned the system she returned to Hawaii where she instructed 22 others in the Reiki system of healing. We, in the West, owe our Reiki heritage to Mrs. Takata.

There are many other systems of Reiki in the world today, as there are lineages. Do not be caught up in either. Reiki is a loving and healing energy with very few rules and regulations. The greatest magnifier of the Reiki energy is LOVE. It is that simple. Usui did not leave a "lineage". He did not leave a manual of Do's and Don'ts. He passed on to his students what worked best for him and allowed them to adapt his teachings to their own. Reiki works well with other modalities. So feel free to add Reiki to any other healing modality that you use.

Reiki energy is transmitted through the hands (and other areas) of an attuned practitioner. This Reiki practitioner is a mere conduit to the passing through of this energy from source. I look at Source as the Creator of everything. That source to be is God. It may be a different name to you, it does not matter. What matters is that you are aware that no energy comes from YOU. In other modalities, the practitioner comes away from giving a treatment drained and/or exhausted. This will never happen with a Reiki treatment. As long as you keep your ego and other healing energies out of the treatment session, the practitioner will feel none of their own personal energy drained from them. It is one of the many things that attracted me to the practice of Reiki.

In other modalities like Qigong use your own accumulation of Qi energy. You must even decide where to amass this energy and when and where to send it. I once went to hear a self proclaimed Qigong master talk about his experiences with using the energy. He talked about his wife who was complaining of a sore throat. He decided that he would use his Qigong energy to help his wife with her sore throat. He gathered up the Qi energy and proceeded to direct that energy directly to her throat. By so doing, he ended up burning her esophagus and had to rush her to the Hospital. This will not happen when you work with Reiki energy. I did not want to use this type of energy in my healing work since I was afraid I would injure a client or my own children. So I began my search for an energy system that I could use that would be safe and effective to use on children. I was lead to the Usui Reiki system of natural healing.

With Reiki, you do not need to worry about giving a client too much energy, Reiki will continue to flow for as long as it is needed and will then "shut off" when the treatment if finished. It takes the guess work out of when, how much, where, until when, etc. Reiki decides where it will go and what it will do and for how long. You are simply supplying the line for which Reiki can make communication to the body. It is truly wonderful!

Chapter Two

Reiki Training - Level One

What You Can Expect from Reiki Level One Training

In a Reiki Level One training session, students are taught the History and Origin of Reiki and its founder, Dr. Mikao Usui. Students are taught hand positions for healing themselves and for healing others.

A typical class will include lectures, discussions, relating of experiences, and attunements. The number of attunements you can expect to receive in a Reiki Level One class differs from Reiki Master to Reiki Master. If this is a concern for you, inquire of your Reiki Master how many attunements you can expect to receive in a Reiki Level One training class. I used to give 4 attunements in one lineage, a second lineage required two, and still another lineage only required one.

Students can also expect to see, and participate in, a total Reiki session. You will also learn techniques such as scanning, beaming, how to do distant healing, and how to incorporate Mudras into your daily life. What I have been made aware of is that not all Reiki masters teach these Reiki techniques. Not all Reiki masters teach the basic Mudras to their students. Perhaps they themselves have not been taught the Mudras and so cannot pass on this information to their students. If this is of a concern to you, you should interview your potential Reiki master and ask what specific things you will be shown and taught in their Reiki classes. Some teachers have a syllabus or content page for their classes; ask them to send you one.

As a potential Reiki student you will have to be a wise and diligent shopper for your Reiki master. You want your Reiki master to be aware of at least the bare minimum of Reiki techniques and hand position. I once had a student that was never shown one single hand position in their Reiki 1 class. How is this possible? If you are not shown the basic hand positions for healing yourself and others in a Reiki class, you better ask the instructor why. All Reiki students should leave a Reiki level 1 training class able to perform a Reiki healing session. Included in this book are several hand positions you can use to heal yourself and others. These hand positions are in no way meant to say these are the only ones you can use. They are not. In the Reiki II and Reiki III books that I have written will be additional hand positions that you may choose to use on yourself and others in the healing session. Do not limit yourself to only what you have been taught. Allow your own intuition to guide your hands where they need to go (respecting your client's boundaries at all times).

After the class, students are expected to continue practicing the Reiki hand positions for healing themselves for a total of at least 21 days. Students will asked to pick a particular time, day or night, where they will be able to do the Reiki hand positions on themselves undisturbed for one hour. This is called the Cleansing Process and is very important for the Reiki practitioner. Students should NOT continue on to Reiki Level Two training until they have completed the Cleansing Process.

What is the Cleansing Process?

After students receive their first Reiki attunement, changes begin to happen within the body. To become clear channels for Reiki healing energy, one must first heal themselves. In fact, in my Reiki Level One training classes, I try to insist that the students work solely on themselves first and complete the 21 Day Cleansing Process, before they go out and attempt to heal others.

By giving yourself daily doses of Reiki energy, you will begin to notice subtle changes taking place. Depending on where you are currently on your spiritual path will determine what type of changes you will notice. The first thing I noticed for myself was that I slept better and felt calmer and more at peace. Yet, the student who had sat right next to me, told horror stories of waking in the middle of night on fire, being moody, trouble sleeping and trouble thinking. I thought that these were pretty dramatic effects from just one attunement. To me, this person needed a lot of clearing of emotional blockages and inner healing.

The more open you are as a channel for this energy, the better the energy will be when you work on someone else. Would you want a healing treatment from the person I mentioned above? I know I sure wouldn't let her touch me. So be aware that the emotions you are feeling can be transmitted to your client. If you are angry, upset, frustrated, chaos is all around you, and then the energy you will be sending to your client will have some of these energies mixed in with it. It can't be helped. My advice to you is to heal yourself and your life and your emotions FIRST before you begin to help others. You may actually do more harm than good if you don't take heed.

Do not be afraid to practice Reiki on yourself for fear of what emotions or experiences you will bring to the service. Know this: you will NEVER be given more that the Universe knows you can handle (and are ready to handle). Know this in your heart and in your mind. The releasing of negative and bottled up emotions is healthy for your body, mind and spirit. Reiki will help you to release those things that do not serve your highest being anymore. Reiki will also help you to heal from the scars these emotions and events have left on your soul. While you are giving yourself your nightly Reiki treatments for the next 21 days, you may find it helpful to jot down a few of your experiences during this Cleansing Process. Journaling is a healthy and healing activity. It will be most helpful for you to express what is happening to you during a Reiki session. I have enclosed a Cleansing Process Journal in the following pages to make this option more easily available to you. Try it for one week and see how it goes.

When writing about your experiences, include any sounds you hear and odors you smell.

Include all of your senses in the viewing of your experiences. What do you see, hear, feel, smell and taste? What stands out most in your images? What fades into the background? What is the overall feeling you are left with? What are your feelings during an image or during the healing session? The more aware you become of the Reiki healing session, the more information you will be able to gather from the session. Don't become discouraged if you don't see anything or feel anything. Time and practice will help you to develop these extra senses of yours so that one day you will be able to. Remember, everyone is able to accomplish this and you will too. Give yourself the time and patience you need in order to do this. It took me two years to learn how to breathe and meditate and accept the extraordinary. If I can do it, so can you.

In the following pages is a Cleansing Process Journal that you can use after you have received your own Reiki attunement. Use this as a time to grow both mentally and spiritually. Many things may come up during your cleansing process, do not become alarmed.

If something comes up during your Cleansing Process, write it down and use this as a time to clear yourself from the attachments you feel to this person, place, or event that comes up. This is a time for your own personal healing. Use this time wisely.

Many practitioners receive such a release from their cleansing process that they feel lighter and free. Some feel that they have had the weight of the world lifted from their shoulders. Others have great insights into their own personal life. Some come away with total understanding and acceptance of situations that have happened in their lives.

However you choose to handle your own personal demons, know that you are not alone. From this cleansing process you will walk away forever changed by the experience. Send Reiki to yourself and to whatever person, place, or event that comes up in your healing process. This is your time to cut all karma cords that are holding you back from being your true higher self. Release all that does not serve you anymore.

Week One – Date:

Day One Notes:

Day Two Notes:

Day Three Notes:

Day Four Notes:

Day Five Notes:

Day Six Notes:

Day Seven Notes:

Cleansing Process Journal

The Second Week-Date:

Day One Notes:

Day Two Notes:

Day Three Notes:

Day Four Notes:

Day Five Notes:

Day Six Notes:

Day Seven Notes:

The Third Week-Date:

Day One Notes:

Day Two Notes:

Day Three Notes:

Day Four Notes:

Day Five Notes:

Day Six Notes:

Day Seven Notes:

Can I Give or Get a Bad Treatment?

The answer is YES! You can give a bad treatment if your energies are scattered. If I am feeling off balance, I will cancel my scheduled appointments before I send them any of that kind of energy. It isn't fair to them and it isn't fair to you to continue with your planned appointments if you know in your heart that you are not up to it. Money isn't everything!

There are very, very, precious few Reiki practitioners (or energy workers in general), that I, myself, would go to for a treatment. I am very sensitive to people's energy fields and the slightest problems that the practitioners may be dealing with could easily throw my own balance off. Remember, when you are receiving a treatment, you are letting your guard (protection) down and allowing the practitioner to work within your energy fields. If you aren't sure about the energy of your practitioner, then you may be stuck. I say, get to know the practitioner first before deciding if this is someone you will want to be in your aura. If in doubt, just play it safe and wait for a treatment. You should also interview other practitioners too. Remember, this is your body and it is up to you to take care of it the best way you know how. If you are concerned about whom you choose to be your doctor and dentist, then you should be equally concerned about choosing your alternative health care practitioner.

How does Reiki differ from other Energy Healing Systems?

There are many things that set Reiki apart from other Energy Healing Systems. Among them are length of training, prior experience, lineage, cost and personal development.

Even though there are three, or four, levels of traditional Reiki training, a student can learn Reiki level 1 and begin practicing Reiki right after the first class. In other systems, you may have to attend several classes in order to gain enough knowledge and ability to perform a healing treatment. Reiki can also be learned as effectively by a five year old as by an adult. For Reiki to flow, one does not need to have any prior experience in working with energy or any other energy system. Students can be of any age and in any physical condition. This means that you can successfully perform a Reiki treatment while confined to a wheel chair or crippled with arthritis. There are many energy healing systems that require you to be in good health and good physical condition before you can be a practitioner. Reiki is not one of them.

I will try to explain the Reiki concept of "lineage". Lineages are unique to the Reiki system of natural healing. Through a lineage, one can trace back all the masters that have gone before them. It is nice to be honoring those who have contributed and enhanced the Reiki energy that has been passed on to you.

I am ever so grateful to each and every master's name that appears on my own lineage. It is how I choose to use my gift of Reiki healing energy that will both enhance and add to the energy of the Reiki I use, or it will detract from it.

Another consideration when looking for an energy system to use is the cost. At one time, Reiki classes were out of reach for most people. At a $10,000 price tag, very few people were able to become Reiki Masters. This of course has all been changed. While you can still attain the lineage containing the $10,000 price tag, you are now free to choose other Reiki Masters who offer their certifications for varying amounts. Each Reiki master charges a different price for their classes and levels of training. You will have to shop around to find a Reiki master in your own area that you can afford. For myself, I offer several different lineage's at different prices. It is of my own choice that I do this. I also offer on-line courses that are less expensive than on-site courses. Some lineage's are not permitted to be done long distance or by correspondence or email. I respect the rights of those Masters and I do not offer those particular courses for long distance learning and certifications. That is also my choice.

And lastly we come to personal development. Receiving the gift of Reiki has literally changed my life. Even though the energy of Reiki is calm and unobtrusive, the results are not. Almost without noticing the small little changes, you wake up one day and see everything in a new light. Reiki works on the cells of your body creating and repairing a new you. It has been one of the most single wondrous events of my life. Through Reiki, colors seem more alive and vibrant. You find yourself wanting to eat healthier, wanting to exercise and honor your body more. You also find yourself repairing broken relationships or finding the courage to finally sever the ties that have been choking and binding you.

Reiki has been many things for many people but the one thing it has always been is "empowering". Through the use of Reiki, we enable ourselves to bring power and control over our own decisions in our lives. And we can now make these tough decisions in love and acceptance.

Reiki works on all levels to bring total health to a person. These levels include the physical, the mental, and the emotional. When someone comes to you for a healing for a stomach ache or pain, you may begin the treatment on the physical level and help ease the pain of the ache. As you continue using Reiki, you find that there were some mental thoughts that went into creating the pain in the stomach. You may also find emotions attached to these aches and pains. Emotions associated with the stomach can be worry. You may pick up that you client is very apprehension. Through talking with your client you can find out what the core issue (or worry) in this case, is and help them to iron out the decisions they need to make to stop the pain from returning. I have had great success stories when clients find the root cause of their problems and ailments and begin to work on them. Reiki helps the client find the means to deal with their core issues. Reiki heals from the outside in, as well as, from the inside out.

Emotions play such a large role in our total health and well being that to be blind to them will not help you or your client. In fact, stress alone is responsible for some 80% of the problems that people face today. Stress causes insomnia, ulcers, back pains, neck pains, and so much more. It only makes sense that if we learn to reduce the stress factors in our life that we can begin to heal our bodies, minds and spirits. Reiki is well known for the benefits it has on stress levels. I can lower my blood pressure by 10 points with one minute of deep breathing and a Reiki treatment.

As in any other system of natural healing, there are no guarantees that one can find the core issue of a problem or that even if you find the core issue of a problem that you can heal from disease. In life, there just are no guarantees. The only thing Reiki can do is to help you help yourself.

Reiki is such a safe and loving energy that you can take it with you wherever you go. You don't need expensive equipment or even a massage table to give a Reiki treatment to someone in need. I have given Reiki treatments to people while they sat in their wheelchairs, laid in their beds at their home, sat on a couch or chair, and even while they lay on the floor. As a Reiki practitioner you must choose what is best for you and the client to facilitate a Reiki treatment.

The Reiki Session

How to perform a Typical Reiki Session

A normal Reiki healing session lasts about one hour. Of course, depending on the situation, it will take what it needs to take. The client will lie on a massage table fully clothed. I usually ask that the client remove their shoes and watch (jewelry optional). Of course, the client may choose to sit in a chair or lie in a bed. All ways are acceptable. You may have a sheet available in case the client feels chilled or you may begin the session by covering them with the sheet from the start. The Reiki energy will run through clothes, even when covered with a sheet.

But before the client even arrives for their healing session, there a few points that I would like you to know. I like to use the time before the client arrives as a time of purification and cleansing. I take a shower and through the use imagery, I imagine standing under a cleansing waterfall that cleanses my aura, my energies, and my physical body.

After the shower, I begin a small cleansing and purification ritual for my healing room. If you are a Reiki II, III, or Master practitioner, you begin by drawing the symbols you will be using in the healing session on each wall, the ceiling, the floor, and on the table itself. (If you want, you can also draw these symbols on the back of your massage table).

For those of you who are Reiki I practitioners, you will then just stand in front of each wall, ceiling, floor, and table and "beam" or "send" Reiki energy for at least 5 minutes.

After I am finished with the room, I then draw the symbols on each of my Chakras, including the Chakras in the palms of my hand. I sit in Gassho meditation to help me focus my intention for the healing session. At this point, any meditation will help you to focus your intention. Breathe slowly and deeply to relax your mind and body.

I am also sure to have a bottle, or glass, of spring water in the room in case I need a drink of water. Nothing is more distracting than running off in the middle of a relaxing session to go fetch a glass of water. I also have a glass, or bottle, of water ready for my client. It has already happened that a client has had a coughing spell in the middle of treatment. I like being prepared. Also, after an hour long healing session, the client will be a bit groggy and need some water to help to revitalize them.

I would just like to interject my own feelings here about the use of smudging and aromatherapy oils in the healing session. Please, ask you clients first before burning incense, diffusing oils, and the like. Your client might have allergies and the last thing you want is for them to have an allergy attack in the middle of a healing session. So, when in doubt, ask.

Last, but not least, be sure that all phones, cell phones, answering machines, and the like are turned off or removed from the room. Imagine how horrible it would feel to be awakened from a calm and relaxing state of healing to the piercing buzz of a telephone ring. This has happened already to me. I had gone for an energy treatment from a friend and halfway into the session, her cell phone rang and she proceeded to answer it and start a conversation. I felt like, "Hey, what about me and my special time". Not only did that cheapen that quality time I had set aside for myself, but it also made me feel that my time was not valued, as a person, and as a client.

Remember to put yourself in your client's place. How would you like to be treated? Then treat your clients the same way.

What does a Reiki Session feel like?

Many people, many experiences. Some people feel Reiki as warmth. Others feel hot energy, cold hands, clammy hands, or even nothing at all. The sensations may even change throughout the course of the treatment. All is acceptable. If they feel nothing at all, it does not mean that they did not receive Reiki. Some people are more sensitive to the energies that are around them, others are not. Every time you set out to give a Reiki treatment, know that you are passing this healing energy onto the client. What the client chooses to do with this energy is up to them, not you.

When we can keep our human ego out of the healing session, the entire session will run more smoothly. Without our ego there are no "Should" or "Shouldn't", no "right" way or "wrong" way. If we remember that each one of us is unique and that each healing session will also be unique, then we can also accept the fact the "we" are not healing anyone. We are merely facilitators to the energy that is called Reiki. And since I believe that Reiki energy will go where it is most needed in the body, then I am also not responsible for the outcomes of a Reiki treatment.

Of course, good and positive feedback is always nice to hear after a Reiki treatment, but in the final analysis, the healing season will be what it is meant to be no matter how we think we can control the outcome.

The Law of Attraction in Reiki:

When someone comes to you, they need you (or they have a lesson for you to learn). This may be baffling at first but this is true. One Reiki practitioner called me complaining about the type of clients she was attracting. "All I seem to attract to me are those people who don't want to work on their issues", she said. So I began to talk to her about what was transpiring in her own life. She soon realized that her clients were mirroring her own need to make decisions for herself in her life. When she began to make the decisions she knew were right for her, her clientele began to change. That is how the Law of Attraction in Reiki works.

For yourself, be alert as to the clients and students you are attracting to yourself. Look to see if there is a common denominator among them. What you find may surprise and enlighten you to what is going on in your own life.

Remember, do not judge or criticize yourself and your clientele. These are all learning lessons and meant to be taken without harsh repercussions.

The First Healing Session:

I like to mentally and physically prepare myself before a healing session. I make sure to remove all jewelry that may interfere with the hand positions and/or be awkward like clanging bracelets, etc. Then I will sit still for a moment and go into a meditative state. I breathe slowly and deeply to reenergize my body's systems and give a little Reiki to myself as I clear my mind of distractions. I center myself for the treatment. You may choose to use the Kanji hand positions at this time. These are described later on in this chapter.

Other things that you should be aware of are:

- Do not force or push the energy, keep your own ego and energy out of it.

- Do not believe that nothing is happening. Something is ALWAYS happening.

- Become detached from the results. Reiki will do what it needs to do.

- Turn over the results to God (or whichever other name Source comes by for you).

- Remember, you cannot make any mistakes with Reiki, you are doing just fine!

- Use your intuition and follow your impressions no matter how weird they may seem.

- Be aware that people need to ask for Reiki healing for it to work in their lives.

- People have free will and they may choose (for whatever reason) NOT to be healed.

- Do not judge your own perception of the flow of energy from your hands.

- Sometimes what you may feel is NOT what the client feels. Keep ego out of it.

What if My Client doesn't feel anything?

There will come times in your Reiki healing sessions where the energy does not seem to flow through into the client. There may be no apparent rhyme or reason for this to happen. Even though you feel that you did all the right preparations and hand positions, you may feel that you did not get the required results. So what happened? Did you somehow lose the ability to channel the energy?

Well, not to worry. You will have your Reiki energy for the rest of your life. You may choose not to use it for years and you will still have it when you need it. It doesn't get up and walk away.

Remember we talked about free will? Well, the client does have the free will to accept or reject the Reiki energy. Even if they come to you and say, "Please do something for me" subconsciously they may be holding on to their illness for whatever reason. It is not your job to discover that reason. It could be a lesson that they need to learn. Until they learn that lesson, they need their dis-ease or ailment. It is a teacher for them. Do not take that away from them. It is not up to you to judge what they need in their lives. Many people cling to their illnesses as a way to control the people around them, or to get attention, or even to get revenge on the happiness of other family members. The reasons are many and varied but the result is all the same. Even if you get are able to rid the body of one dis-ease, another will come and take its place. The lesson must be learned first and/or the client must be willing to let it go.

Other times, clients need to prove it to themselves that Reiki would never work on their condition - that it hopeless. They block the flow of energy in their body and resist it at every turn. For them, nothing will work until they choose to allow it to happen. So what can you do?

As Reiki practitioners there is only one thing you can do. You will provide your client with information about your Reiki practice and offer them the possibility of what the treatment may do for them. Do not force them into a treatment. Just do your work well, make no attachments to the outcome, pour out love and understanding that they are where they need to be in their lives at that moment, and simply remain open to whatever may occur now, or in the future, with them. You may be surprised at the clients who will return years down the line for follow up treatments all because you were open, fair, accepting, and loving. They will not forget that you gave them the respect to be where they needed to be at that time in their life.

Chapter Three

Other Uses for Reiki Energy

Food and Drink

I use the Reiki energy while I prepare meals (especially when stirring or mixing foods). I even give Reiki energy to the water that I drink. You can do this by holding the glass of water in your hands and sending Reiki to it for a few minutes before drinking it. In fact, one of the exercises that you can do to prove to yourself how Reiki changes the molecules structures of water is this:

Exercise 1:

Take a sip of water from the glass right now. Swirl the water in your mouth and around your tongue. Make a note of how this water feels in your mouth, its texture and taste. Write down your observations here:

_____

_____

_____

_____

_____

_____

_____

Exercise 2:

Now, hold the water glass or bottle in your hands and send Reiki energy into the glass or bottle for 5 minutes. Take a sip of water from the glass that has just received Reiki energy. See if you can taste a difference. Write down your observations here:

_____

_____

_____

_____

_____

_____

_____

For most people, they will taste a more metallic taste to the water. Other students have said the water felt lighter in their mouths. Depending on the water you use, you may actually taste something quite different. This little exercise is just to show you whether there is a difference at all.

You can give the food you eat energy by placing your hands over the pot while cooking or when you place the food on the dish, holding your hand, or hands, over the plate. You can Reiki the plate before putting the food on it. You can hold the glass in between your two hands and channel energy.

Exercise 3

When you sit down to your next meal, I want you to try this little exercise. Take a taste of your food and be aware of how you feel eating the food, as well as, how the food tastes and feels in your body. Now, place your hands 2" above your food and close your eyes. Breathe in through your nose air mixed with Reiki energy. Connect to the Reiki energy with your mind and your intent. Feel that Reiki energy flowing into your body and into your hands and into the food. Continue this exercise for at least one minute. Now, taste your food again. Has your feelings about eating this food changed? Has the taste of the food itself changed? Has the feeling of the food in your body changed? Write down your observations here:

(Please note that if you did not feel or sense anything different do not worry. Sensations will come with time and practice.)

_____

_____

_____

_____

_____

_____

_____

_____

Medicines and Ointments

I hold all medicines, ointments, salves, etc. in between my hands and send Reiki energy into them before either I or my family uses them. You may even use them on prescription medications if you choose. It does not affect the validity or potency of the drug.

Environment

After my Level I Reiki training, I went home and proceeded daily to use my Reiki on everything in my house. I started in one room and sent Reiki energy to every corner; ceiling, floor, couch, statue, picture, and knick knack. Sending Reiki energy in this way changes the whole "feel" of the room. It was also a way for me to appreciate the things that I did have. I gave each item its own Reiki energy. I would look at that item, remember why I had purchased it and for what purpose it had served in my life. It was a truly loving experience. Afterward, I would go outside and Reiki my car, the outside of my house, and other items that were generally kept outside. Everything that I owned eventually received the Reiki energy. Remember, the more you use Reiki, the stronger it becomes. I had definite goals on changing my life.

Assignment

Go into your home now and hold your most valued possessions in your hand and send them the loving Reiki energy. Include your home and car in this assignment and write down your feelings both before giving Reiki and after you completed giving Reiki energy.

_____

_____

_____

_____

_____

_____

_____

_____

_____

Jewelry

You can place your jewelry, either individually or together, in the palms of your hands and send Reiki energy into them (Except for watches). For some reason, I seem to stop watches, so I would avoid this if possible. However, after I became a Reiki master I was finally able to "attune" my watches so that I can wear them again without them stopping in one day.

Assignment:

Take off the jewelry you are wearing right now and place them in your non dominant hand. Place your dominant hand over your jewelry and begin sending Reiki energy into your jewelry for 5 minutes. Report your experiences here:

_____

_____

_____

_____

_____

_____

_____

Crystals and gemstones

Instead of all the rules and regulations required for proper gemstone and crystal clearing and cleansing, I now use only Reiki energy and Intent on clearing my crystals. It works beautifully, easily, and naturally.

Assignment:

If you own any crystals or gemstones, place them in your non dominant hand and place your dominant hand over them and send Reiki energy to them for at least 5 minutes. If you have a rather large collection of crystals and gemstones, then place them in front of you on the floor or table. Position your hands 2"-4" above your collection and begin to send them Reiki energy for at least 5 minutes. Report on your sensations and discoveries here:

_____

_____

_____

_____

_____

Many people have reported feeling the crystals and gemstones responding to the Reiki energy. Some students can feel the crystals and gemstones "pulse", or heartbeat, in their hands. Other students can hear a hum coming from the stones. Still other students feel other responses coming from their collection. It is a positive and loving experience.

There is no right or wrong experience. Whatever you feel, even if it is nothing at all, it perfect and right for you right here, right now. Be patient with yourself, it will all happen in its own right time and its own right way.

Treating Plants with Reiki Energy

Reiki energy can be used on plants with great success. In fact, this is a very easy way for those who are new to Reiki to continue to practice their gift without feeling awkward or embarrassed to work on other people. If you feel unsure of your abilities and want to practice to gain your confidence in your newly acquired gift, then plants are a great client. They won't criticize or judge and they are so grateful for the energy!

There is no right way or wrong way in which to transmit the Reiki energy to a plant. I have listed just some ideas that I myself have used and I will leave the rest up to you. One method of transmitting Reiki energy into a house plant, or a plant that is in a small pot, is to place that pot on your lap and hold between your hands. You can then begin to send Reiki energy into that pot. If the plant is too large to sit on your lap, then you can leave it where it is and you can put your hands on the pot and transmit Reiki energy into it.

Another method that can be used on trees is to wrap your arms around a tree and send it Reiki energy. If the tree is too large, you can then place your two hands on the tree and send it Reiki energy. Still another method is to stand in front of the plant, or an area of plants, that you intend to send Reiki energy to and use the beaming method of sending Reiki to "beam" or "send" the Reiki energy to that plant or area of plants.

There is a plane of energy-consciousness where you can feel the gratitude that the plants send you as their way of thanking you for the Reiki energy. Try to become aware of this consciousness. When I send Reiki energy to my herbs, they send off an aroma to me that surround me and I can feel the gratitude and appreciation that comes from them. After all, they are alive.

You can even use Reiki energy to help cut flowers stay fresh longer. Just put your hands on the vase and send Reiki energy into the water, or stand in front of the vase and send, or beam, Reiki energy into the cut flowers themselves.

When you have obtained the symbols from Second Degree Reiki, you will be able to do absentee healing with the plants and have great success in doing so. This technique will work great when you are interested in sending Reiki healing energy into a grove or forest of trees.

I remember watching my young son when he was 8 years old work with my plants. One plant had leaves that were literally dropping downward. He took his hands and cradled the leaves and sent them Reiki energy. You could stand there and watch as each leaf began to rise up off his hands and reach skyward. It was truly amazing. To this day I regret not having a video camera to record that event.

Assignment

Take one of your potted plants, or cut flowers in a vase, and hold them between both of your hands. Send Reiki energy into the plant or flowers for 5 minutes and report on your findings.

_____

_____

_____

_____

_____

_____

Treating Animals with Reiki

As with plants, Reiki energy can also be used on animals. The same life force energy that is in us runs through all living things. And that includes plants and animals. In fact, animals love the Reiki energy. Animals are extremely receptive and accepting of this form of energy work. They respond exceedingly well.

In fact, when I would give my Reiki attunements or have a Reiki share at my home, the blue herons and egrets would flock to the window to enjoy some of the Reiki energy. It was like they knew that we were working with the Reiki energy and they wanted to share in some of it.

Here are some methods you can use to share the gift of Reiki with your pets. Remember, there is no right way or wrong way with giving them Reiki energy. In fact, one way would be to try and duplicate the hand positions for healing yourself and using that on your pets. One word of caution though, like children, some pets attention span is very short. Do not become discouraged if your pet will only sit still for a few minutes before running off. Be aware that some pets do not want Reiki energy and if they think you have an intention to give them some, they will run off and hide. Please, don't force a pet into receiving Reiki energy. When they are in need of it, they will come to you and ask for it.

For some students, every time they begin to practice their Reiki energy, they can't get their pets to leave them alone. Some pets are so into Reiki energy that they will stay with you the entire time you are practicing it.

Another method you can use on animals is the beaming method. You can stand in front of the animal and beam them Reiki energy. This method works wonderful if you see a wild animal that has been hurt. I use this method also when birds are flying overhead and when I go to the aquariums or nature trails.

For fish, I just place my hands on either side of the aquarium and send Reiki energy into the tank. I used this method when we had purchased a new fish tank and one of our larger fishes was acting hysterical to the new space. I sent Reiki energy into the tank along with the thought of peace and calmness and within minutes the fish calmed down. The fish is now quite happy and content in its new environment.

You can place your pet on your lap, or you can sit down on the floor with your pet to give them a Reiki treatment. In fact, you don't need to use all the hand positions on your pet. Just placing two hands on your pets back with do the trick.

If your pet has a particular health problem, you can place your hands directly on that area (if safe to do so), or leave your hands a few inches above that area and send Reiki energy into it.

One method of animal healing is to lay your hands directly behind the ears of the pet and send Reiki energy for a few minutes. Then you will lift your hands off your pet and proceed to the afflicted area, or areas, of the animal's body. You will then send energy to these areas. Having your hands behind the animals' ears is said to calm them down. Try this for yourself and see what happens.

There is no set time for how long a Reiki treatment will last when working with a pet. The session will last as long as the pet sits still for it, or as long you feel that it is necessary. Each session is unique. Your pet may be all over you for a Reiki treatment one day and run away from you the next. They know if they need Reiki energy so let them decide when they want a session and how long they want the session to last. In fact, I have attuned Reiki students who actually came for the training not for themselves, but for their pets.

I also believe in attuning pets to the Reiki energy. This may cause so discern in the Reiki community at large, but then again, it is my choice and it feels right to me. Some pets are such natural healers that I can see nothing wrong with attuning them to Reiki. I have been asked in the past to attune some pets to Reiki and I have done so. Of course, I don't go so far as to give them a certification or lineage, only the gift of Reiki to share with others.

Assignment

Using your own willing pet, or neighbors, sit with the pet and send it Reiki energy for 5 minutes (you can send Reiki energy longer if the pet is willing). Report on both your experience as sending the energy and your observations of your pet after they have received the energy.

_____

_____

_____

_____

_____

_____

_____

_____

_____

The Reiki Box

What is a Reiki Box?

    A Reiki Box is another method used to sending healing energies. This box can either be hand made by the practitioner or purchased in any store. Your Reiki box can be decorated with fancy beads or left plain. Some Reiki students paint the Reiki symbols on the outside and/or inside of the box. Other students decorate the box with colorful gemstones and crystals. There is no one right way or wrong way to decorate you Reiki box. The design is up to you. There are also many ways to use your Reiki box.

    One way to use your Reiki box is to write on a piece of paper a person or event to which you would like to send Reiki healing energy. Then place that piece of paper between your hands and send Reiki energy in to the piece of paper for 5 minutes. Place the piece of paper into the box and send Reiki energy into the box. You can hold the box between your hands if you want to, or just place your hands on the box and send the box Reiki energy. Then, for the next 7 days (or until a healing has taken place or a specific outcome has been achieved) you will send Reiki energy into the box every time you pass by it. You can send Reiki energy into the box several times throughout the day. This is very loving and very powerful. It helps to keep you focused on the desired outcome and helps you to learn to channel your energy in a focused manner.

Chapter Four

The Hands in Reiki

How to Hold your Hands

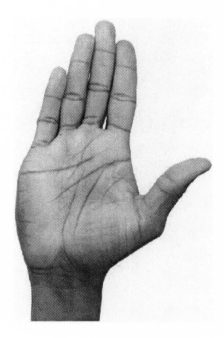

It is commonly taught to students that when performing your hand positions, you should strive to keep your fingers together. Not only are students encouraged to keep their fingers together, they are also encouraged to keep their hands cupped. Some people believe that when your fingers are opened you are dispersing energy out from them. Those types of exercises are used in Yoga classes for releasing tensions in the body.

It is also believed that you can better focus and gather energy when your fingers are closed together and your hands are slightly cupped. Some lineages require their students to keep their hands perfectly flat, not cupped. As far as what I teach, I encourage my students to do what feels right for them. If you feel comfortable in a certain hand position, then use that hand position.

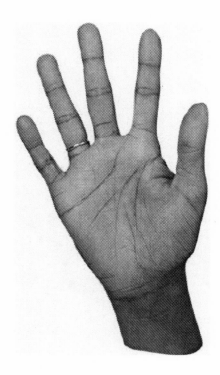

In the picture above the fingers are apart. This is said to disperse energy. Actually, this is another technique that we will discuss in other Reiki levels of training - the dispersing of energy. For now, try to practice your hand positions with your fingers closed. Concentrate on the energy that is coming from your hands and set your intention before, during and after each Reiki session.

Chapter 5

The Endocrine System

What is the Endocrine System?

While giving Reiki in the Healing Session, it is the aim of every Reiki practitioner to channel the Reiki energy throughout the whole body of the client. Helpful to the practitioner would be a knowledge of the Endocrine System and a basic understanding of it's function.

The Endocrine System is made up of several glands.

They are:

The Pituitary

The Pineal

The Thyroid and Parathyroid

The Thymus

The Islets of Langerhans (Pancreas)

The Adrenals

The Gonads (in men)/The Ovaries (in women)

It is the job of the Endocrine System to secrete chemicals called hormones via the bloodstream. This in turn helps to regulate the body's organs and tissues. These hormones help the body to fight off infections and are essential for reproduction. When the Endocrine System is not functioning many problems occur within the body. Some of these imbalances are: diabetes, thyroid problems, infertility, etc. Once hormones are out of balance, it is not easy to rebalance them. Stress takes a major toll on our hormones also. We seem to be constantly under stress and it wears the body's system down.

Mrs. Takata taught hand positions that took into account the entire Endocrine System. In Reiki, we make a connection between the healing energies of Reiki and the physical body of the client. Medical science has a hard time understanding this connection due to the fact that is cannot be scientifically measured on any machine. Those who work with this system however, know it be real.

There are said to be 7 hand positions for the Endocrine System. These hand positions, for some, are all that is required for a total body treatment.

But before you begin the hand positions for the Endocrine System, I would like to discuss the Chakra system with you. This will be only a basic understanding of each of the 7 major Chakra systems in the body and include basic information of the organs, emotions, and other systems related to that Chakra. You can use this knowledge to help build a protocol for future healing sessions with your client. Remember, it is not legal for you to practice medicine without a license. If you are NOT a medical doctor, or otherwise licensed and trained, you may NOT diagnose a condition nor may you suggest a treatment for your client to follow.

While it is not necessary for a Reiki Practitioner to have a full understanding of the Endocrine System, or any other system of the human body, I found it to be of great interest and help in my own Reiki practice. As long as a Reiki practitioner does a complete body treatment, they can be assured of covering the entire major, and many of the minor, organs of the human body. Reiki does not need you to direct the flow of energy. It will go exactly where it is needed.

The Endocrine System and the Chakras

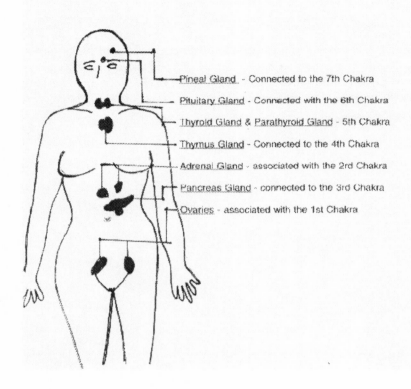

Pineal Gland - Connected to the 7th Chakra

Pituitary Gland - Connected with the 6th Chakra

Thyroid Gland & Parathyroid Gland - 5th Chakra

Thymus Gland - Connected to the 4th Chakra

Adrenal Gland - associated with the 2nd Chakra

Pancreas Gland - connected to the 3rd Chakra

Ovaries - associated with the 1st Chakra

Hand Positions for the Endocrine System

Hand Position #1

The Eyes

This hand position deals with the Bladder, Stomach, and Gall bladder. While doing this hand position you will also be including the Pineal Gland and the Pituitary Gland. The area associated with this hand position will also benefit the Thyroid Gland and the Parathyroid Gland.

Hand Position #2

The Temples

This hand position deals with the Gall bladder and Triple Warmer meridian. Also benefiting from this hand position is the Pineal and Pituitary Gland.

Hand Position #3

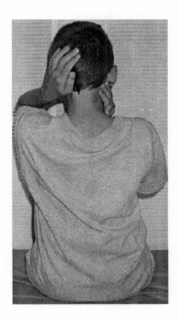

Occipital

This hand position is for the Gallbladder meridian. Also benefiting from this hand position is the Pineal and Pituitary Gland.

Hand Position #4

Clavicle

This hand position is for the Stomach and Gallbladder. Using this hand position will also benefit the Thyroid and Parathyroid glands. You can use this hand position to benefit the Thymus gland.

Hand Position #5

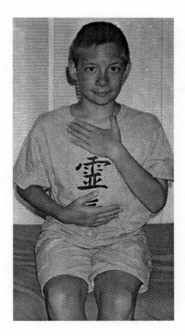

Lower Ribs

This hand position is used for the Liver meridian. Using this hand position will also benefit the Heart meridian. You can use this hand position for benefiting the lung meridian. The Pancreas and adrenal glands are also included in this hand position. This hand position is also associated with the Stomach meridian and includes the small and large intestine.

Hand Position #6

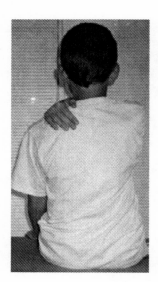 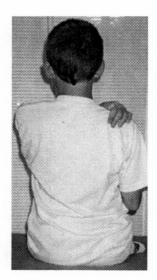

Shoulders

This hand position includes the Small Intestine and Gall bladder meridians. The body's temperature system is located in this area. This position will also benefit the Pituitary gland.

Hand Position #7

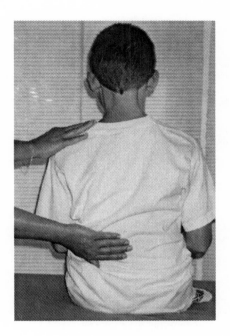

Lower Back

This hand position includes the Kidneys and the Bladder. Using this hand position will also help the Reproductive system and meridian. Use this position for the Urinary system.

Chapter Six

The Chakra System

What is a Chakra?

A Chakra is a Sanskrit word meaning, "wheel", or "wheel of light". Each Chakra is seen as spinning in a circular movement and in a specific direction. Each Chakra spins at a different rate of speed. The speed will depend upon many factors such as the health and over all vitality of the individual. The greater the health and vitality, the faster the Chakra spins.

Each Chakra is a center of energy and is recognized to its relationship with the physical, emotional, mental, and spiritual energy systems of the body. Each Chakra has its own name, color, mantra, element, sound, and more. The whole purpose of studying the Chakra system is to help us integrate wholeness within ourselves. We can then bring the physical, mental, emotional, and subconscious aspects of health into our lives.

We can see that if we feel a certain way, our emotions may actually make us sick. For instance, if you are a very angry person, this anger may translate into a heart condition such as a heart attack.

The Seven Major Chakras of the Human body system are:

Root

Sacral

Solar Plexus

Heart

Throat

Brow

Crown

There are several minor chakras located throughout the body. The ones we use most are:

Center of the Palm of the Hands

Fingertips

Center of the Sole of the Feet

The 7 Major Chakras

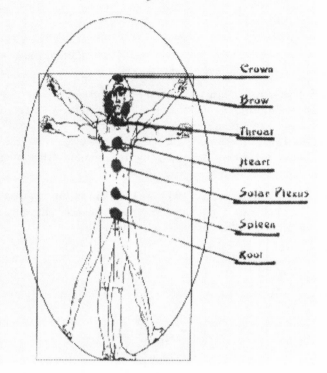

Crown

Brow

Throat

Heart

Solar Plexus

Spleen

Root

Chakra #1 - The Root

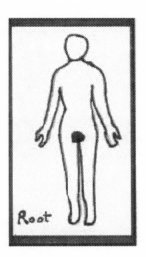
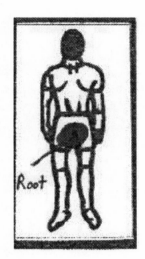

     The Root Chakra is also known as the Base Chakra or the Red Chakra. I will usually interchange the words Root and Base throughout this book. Just be aware that when I do, I am speaking of the same Chakra.

     The Root Chakra is located at the base of the spine (front and back). It is said to govern the adrenal gland and is the sense of smell. It is the place of birth & rebirth.

     This Chakra deals with familial beliefs, superstitions, loyalty, instincts, physical pain, physical pleasure, and the human touch. This Chakra gives you the ability to draw abundance from the universe. The spiritual lesson to be learned from the Root Chakra is that of material world lessons.

     People who worry about money, food, job security, etc. will have a very active or closed Chakra area. A balanced Chakra will allow you freedom from such worries for you will be able to ask the universe for something that is needed and receive it.

The Root Chakra is the "right to have". It is also the "right to be here". It concerns itself with all the basic needs to survive on this planet. Food, clothing, money, home, warmth, health, and even your human freedoms are all associated with this Chakra.

This Chakra includes the base of the spine, coccyges plexus, large intestine, legs, knees, calves, feet and even the toes. Client's suffering from the following conditions can be helped through this center: obesity, spaciness, hemorrhoids, constipation, bone disorders, frequent illnesses, fears, inability to focus, knee problems, feet problems, leg problems, diarrhea, eating disorders, sciatica, restlessness, poor circulation, and varicose veins.

This Chakra center is associated with the following emotions: anger, hatred, self loathing, racism, revenge, envy sloth, impulsiveness, violent nature, listlessness, edgy, obsessive behaviors, boredom, inaction, giving up, maliciousness, complacency, laziness, autism, dishonesty, insecurity, fear, threat to survival issues, lack of trust or trust issues,

Positive qualities associated with this Chakra include: self-esteem, justice and a sense of fair play, love, family, community, gratitude, equality, fortitude, charity, trust, spontaneity, activity, display of leadership skills, ability to be grounded and to be present in the here and now.

Chakra #2 - Sacral

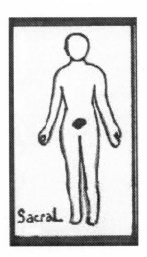
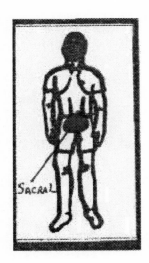

The Second Chakra is called the Sacral Chakra. It is also known as the Orange Chakra, the Spleen Chakra, and the Navel Chakra. This Chakra center is the center for sexual energy and pure emotion. It governs sexuality, creativity, emotions such as anger, fear, and perceptions concerning food and sex. This Chakra is our ability and right to feel.

When this Chakra is in balance, it provides us with an ease in sharing our emotions with others and sharing the needs of others. We have a positive body awareness of ourselves which results in positive self-esteem. We are able to create and express our individuality and healthy sexuality easily and safely (without harm to others-such as in rape).

When out of balance, one suppresses the expression of natural needs resulting in feelings of inadequacy, possessiveness, jealousy, envy, and self regret on all levels. Anti-social behaviors, lustfulness, selfishness and arrogance all stem from an imbalance in this Chakra center.

Also included in this Chakra are other emotions such as the need to control, addictions, shame, guilt, desire, humorlessness, homophobia, disobedience, pride, egoism, sadomasochism, violence, thoughtlessness, hatred, despair of the future, victimization, masochism, sentimentalism, and consumerism (the need for more stuff).

This Chakra is associated with the spleen in men and the uterus in women. Impotency, infertility, frigidity, diabetes, kidney problems, bladder problems, reproductive problems, and muscular system problems are all helped with this center.

This center also deals with repressed emotions, comfort, and inner strength.

Chakra #3 - Solar Plexus

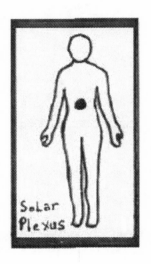

The Third Chakra is known as the Solar Plexus Chakra and is also called the Yellow Chakra. It is located 2" above the navel. This Chakra holds our formed personality, our wishes and desires. It is where our strength and ability to take action lay. It is our vague sense of knowingness, our oneness and focus of mind.

The Solar Plexus Chakra is our Personal Power center. Our self motivation stems from this center. Here we make the decisions in our life. This center houses our willfulness and our self-image. It is our sense of sight and the element of fire.

Greed, doubt, anger, powerlessness, and guilt are all associated with this center. When out of balance in this center, one restricts the acceptance of the natural flow of the Universe, creating a tendency for needing material reinforcement here are the extroverts, inflated egos, power hungry, your will over others, power, and angers simmer. Lethargy, feelings of isolation, nervousness, distrust, and psychic overload all occur in this center.

When properly functioning, one has "gut" instincts of what to do in any given situation. A person with a properly balanced Solar Plexus Chakra will possess an inner calm and tolerance for the world around them. These people will also have high regards and self-esteem. They will also possess the ability to generate abundance through creative visualization of their goals through the power of manifesting.

On a physical level, this Chakra deals with issues of food and its assimilation into the body. It also deals with how the body digests the food it consumes and how the body distributes this food. Here is where digestive problems begin.

The negative attributes of this Chakra system include alcoholism, rage, violence, anger, destructive behaviors, bitterness, fury, insecurity, wrath, bickering, passive-aggressive behavior, victimization (the surrendering of our power to others).

The diseases and illnesses associated with this Chakra include: Ulcers, jaundice, hepatitis, hypoglycemia, gall stones, skin problems, skin diseases, pancreas, nerves, nervous system, pancreas, gall bladder, intestines, and diabetes.

Chakra #4 - Heart

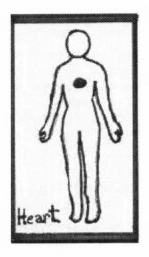 

The Fourth Chakra is known as the "Heart Chakra". It has also been called the "Green Chakra", and the "Pink Chakra". It is located in the center of the chest and is considered the "center" of the Chakra system.

This center provides the ability to love freely and unconditionally. It controls the creative process and is where our sense of "wholeness" originates. A balance between the spiritual and the physical is located here. In the Heart Chakra our life force in anchored. Through this Chakra center, our immune system is strengthened. This center governs the concept of love, how we love, who we love, and why we love. Our compassion stems from this center. It is our sense of touch.

When this center is out of balance we feel restricted in our own ability to give and receive love to both ourselves and to others. Low self-esteem, insecurity, jealousy, feeling unloved, stinginess, self doubting, "martyr" syndrome, and the "poor me" syndrome are all associated with this Chakra. When out of balance, the flow of energy is restricted to all the other Chakras.

Fear, avarice, resentments, greed, pride, self pity, betrayal, blame, pessimism, sarcasm, anxiety, perjury, fraud, treachery, deceit, and hardness of heart are found in this center. Moral outrage, compassion, mercy, forgiveness, love, satisfaction, gratitude, and also compassion are some of the emotions attached to this Chakra center.

This Chakra center is also associated with the thymus, heart, blood, circulatory system, glands, lungs, cardiac plexus, and the pericardium.

Diseases and ailments connected to this Chakra center include: Arthritis, respiratory problem, cardiac problems, stroke, hypertension, nervous headaches, emotional disorders, asthma, allergies, blood pressure, lungs, tissue degeneration, relationship problems, sleep disorders, bronchitis, pneumonia, co dependency issues, caretaking issues, and AIDS.

Chakra #5 - Throat

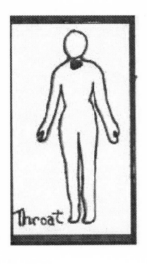
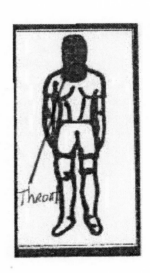

The Fifth Chakra, known as the "Throat Chakra", may also be called the "Blue Chakra". Located at the base of the throat, this Chakra allows us to transform our emotions into healthy creative expressions such as painting, writing, dancing, singing, etc. It is our ability to express ourselves, our beliefs, our feelings and ideas into acceptable forms of communication.

The Throat Chakra is our ability to surrender to others. It governs our speech, hearing and communication of self expression. This Chakra is our sense of our own inner voice, our own inner truth. It is the beginning seat of our intuition. It is the sense of healing and the element of ether.

This Chakra center empowers us to speak the truth, our truth, and to allow others their own voice. It is the truth of one's heart. It governs our "inner ear" and our telepathy. It is also responsible for our feelings of youthfulness and longevity.

When in balance, one would feel an inner peace. You would feel strength in your convictions, in your truths, in yourself. This is not the strength that comes from physical power, but a strength that comes from an inner knowing in yourself, or your divine self.

Organs associated with the Throat Chakra include" Throat, vocal chords, esophagus, mouth, teeth, thyroid, parathyroid, respiratory system, laryngeal plexus, and the cervical spine. Communications, expression, creativity, interactions and inspiration all flow from this center.

When out of balance one may have feelings of: fear of judgment, fear of rejection, negative speaking, criticizing, over acting, hyperactive attitudes, gluttony, consumerism, shopping addictions and emotional excess. You may also have a tendency to shut up the youth, or suffer from drug addictions (this includes smoking, drinking and over eating), greed of food, greed of things, concealing and/or hiding the truth, obsession, stagnation, lying, hypocrisy, lack of expression, withheld words (biting your tongue), inability to express ideas or words to others, stubborn beliefs, domineering words, and communication problems

Diseases and Ailments associated with this energy center include: Sore throats, voice problems, thyroid problems, flu, vertigo, anemia, allergies, fatigue, asthma, bronchial and vocal problems, fevers and laryngitis.

Chakra #6 - Brow

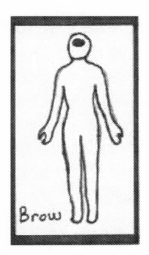

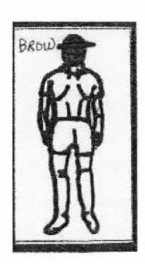

The sixth Chakra is known as the "Brow Chakra". Other names for this Chakra center are, "Third Eye Chakra", "Indigo Chakra", and the "Ajna Center". This Chakra is located one finger width above the bridge of the nose at the center of the forehead. This center represents the concept of "being" and "existence". This center belongs to the spiritual world.

It is from this center that we project our dreams outwards into the physical realm. This is where our source of intuition, insight, and clairvoyance stem. It is our Physic Perception. It is all the elements. It is here that we are provided with a sense of spirituality, intuition, and inner awareness of self. Our intuition is governed here through inner and outer sight, visions, and dreams. The colors associated with this Chakra are indigo, violet, and/or yellow.

When this Chakra is out of balance one may experience the following emotions: Self doubt, injustice, cruelty, inner guilt, forgetfulness, inability to trust our instincts, sadism, ignorance, greed, avarice, stifles wisdom, stifles creativity, stifles prophetic dreams, and superstitious.

When in balance, one would experience emotions such as: creativity, truth, strength, the sharing of ourselves, the sharing of your time with others, the sharing of your needs with others, the sharing of your ideas with others, the sharing of your hopes with others, and the sharing of your fears with others. You will be open to possibilities. You would not stay blind to what is around you. You will have a union with the angels in your lives and be more open to the seen, as well as, the unseen.

Organs and ailments associated with this Chakra include: sinus problems, congested head, ear diseases and problems, eye diseases and problems, nose diseases and problems, mental problems, head conditions, skeletal system, sleep disorders and problems, pituitary gland, nervous system, pineal gland, headaches, and fuzzy thinking.

Chakra #7 - Crown

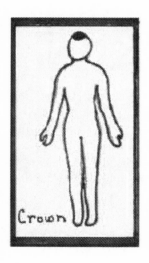 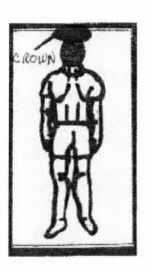

The seventh Chakra is the "Crown Chakra". Also known as the "Violet Chakra", the "White Chakra", the "Gold Chakra", and the "All is One" Chakra. It is the "Spirit Center" of the body. It is located at the top of the head and slightly to the back.

This center allows us to surmount self limiting thoughts and provides us with the sense of Oneness and Unity with the Divine. It is the connection to the cosmic consciousness, it is spiritual, and it is wisdom. It holds our aspirations and the knowledge of the truth. It reflects our ability to receive light from the source. It is our connection to our higher self and astral travel. It is all the elements, it is cosmic. Through this center we must learn to release, to surrender our will.

When out of balance one would feel emotions such as: anxiety, fear, disconnection with the oneness, feelings of being misunderstood, uninspired, feelings of hatred, gossip, envy, resentments, sorrows, gloom, peer pressure, mob mentality, happy over another's misfortune, self denial, being impractical and being over imaginative.

When in balance, you would experience emotions such as: Understanding, speaking only words of love and encouragement, taking no pleasure in another's downfall, united to different realms and worlds, strengthens the heart for the struggle, lends spiritual support for our journey, spiritual wisdom and interconnectedness.

Ailments and organs associated with this Chakra include: insomnia, epilepsy, pain, nervous problems, rheumatism, neuralgia, brain tumors, cerebral tumors, cranial pressure, depression, insanity, confinement, psychosis, worry, and closed mindedness.

Chapter Seven

Reiki Methods and Techniques

Scanning

(1) Body Scanning

We can use this technique to gain valuable information from the client's body before beginning a healing session. You will have your client lie on a massage table and you will stand to the side of your client (it doesn't matter whether you stand on the left or right side of your client). You will position both of your hands 4" above the physical body of your client. Starting at your client's head, you will slowly move your hands from 4" above the top of your client's forehead down their body to their feet and slowly back up their body returning to your starting position 4" above your client's forehead.

You will lower your hands to about 2" above your client's body and you will repeat this scanning technique down their body to their feet and back up their body returning to the starting position 2" above their forehead.

What you are doing is gathering information on the energy signatures that the client's body is giving off. As you were passing your hands slowly down the client's body, did you feel areas of intense heat, or cold? Did you feel dips and valleys? Did you feel tingling sensations? Were you drawn in to certain areas and repelled at other areas?

These are only a few examples of what you, as a Reiki practitioner, may experience in a typical body scan. Do not become discouraged if you feel nothing at all after a body scan. With practice and patience, you will begin to notice the subtle changes in the auric field that surrounds your client. You will also learn what certain sensations mean in the body. Here are some of my own observations in this area. Remember, these observations may be right for me but not for you. You will have to go on your own fact finding mission to find out what these sensations mean to you.

Energy Sensations You May Experience and what they Mean

Intense Heat

Whenever I pass an area of intense heat it is a signal to me that this area both needs and wants Reiki energy. I place my hands on this area (if appropriate) and send Reiki energy into this area until I feel the heat dissipate.

Intense Cold

Whenever I come across an area of intense cold it is a signal to me that this person is suffering from an emotional blockage. This blockage may be deep seated or may have just happened recently. Whatever the reason, this blockage is keeping this person from total well being and needs to be addressed. You may try talking about this issue with your client to bring the emotions out into the open so that they may be healed.

Tingling

Tingling sensations on the tips of the fingers can be subtle like the feeling you get when your hand falls asleep, or can be extremely painful as if the tips of knives are being poked into your fingers. When I sense tingling, it is a signal to me that the client is suffering from an infection, or an inflammation, in that area. The about of discomfort that I am feeling is usually telling me how severe this infection or inflammation is in the client's body.

I once was working on a woman and had to stop the treatment because the pain was so intense that I could no longer put my hands on her to work on her. I told her squarely that she needed to go to the doctors and have herself checked out immediately. She went and was diagnosed with cancer. The disease had spread to her lymph system and lungs.

Repelling

Feelings of being repelled away from a client is usually signaling to me that this person does not want the Reiki energy in this area and does not want me to interfere with what is going on inside. When I experience this sensation I just continue on with the treatment with the next hand position.

Magnetizing

Sometimes you may experience the sensation of being drawn into a particular area of a client's body. This is a signal that this area is in dire need of Reiki energy. Just go ahead and place your hands in this are (if appropriate) and send Reiki energy into this area until the feeling goes away.

Assignment 1:

Take your hands and place them 2-4" off your body with palms of the hands facing your body. Now, starting at the top of your head slowly pass your hands over the front of your body. If you can reach your feet, continue the body scans down to your feet. If you are able to reach your feet, just pass your hands over your body as far as you can reach. Write down your findings here:

_____

_____

_____

_____

_____

_____

Assignment 2:

Find yourself a volunteer and have them rest in a comfortable position. Pass your hands 4" off their body starting at the top of their head and continue down to underneath their feet and back up again. Write down your findings. Then pass your hands 2" above their body starting at the top of their head and continue down to underneath their feet and back up again. Now, have your volunteer turn over and repeat the body scans to the back of their body. Write down your findings here:

_____

_____

_____

_____

_____

_____

2. Aura Scanning

Remember we talked about the energy that surrounds us all? This is called the aura. The aura is made up of many layers and many colors. We are not going to get into a big discussion here about auras. I am only bringing this up so that you may be aware that you can use the same techniques you used for body scanning for scanning the aura as well.

To scan the aura, you will lift both your hands about 3' off your client's body. I slowly and deliberately begin lowering both of hands and stop 2" above the client's body. When I reach that point, I lift my hands off the body and shake them out. Then I lift both of my hands again 3' above the client's body and this time I am in a new location. I continue to lower my hands through the layers of aura and when I reach 2" above the client's body, I remover my hands and shake them out. I like to start at the head of the client and work down to the feet. This is my preference and you can choose whatever way works best with you.

You will be surprised at some of the sensations you may feel in the aura. You may actually encounter shapes of substance, tingling sensations, warmth, coldness, wholes and tears. There are many books out on the market with techniques on dealing with balancing the aura.

One note here is this, Reiki was never taught to work in the aura. I know that I use it in my own healing session but if you do not believe in auras, do not let this stop you from becoming a Reiki practitioner. This technique is just something that I, myself, have added to the Reiki healing session. Don't ever feel pressured into using techniques and methods that do not resonate with you.

Assignment:

Find a volunteer and have them lie, or sit, in a comfortable position. Begin with your hands 3' above their body and slowly bring your hands to 2-4" above their physical body. Lift your hands off the body and repeat in another area of the body. I like to start at the top of the head and move down the body for a total of at least 10 passes. When finished with the front of your volunteer, have them turn over (if they were lying down) and work on the back of their aura in the exact same way that you worked on their front. Write your findings here:

_____

_____

_____

_____

_____

Additional Notes:

_____

_____

_____

_____

_____

Beaming

What is Beaming?

Beaming is a technique used in the First Level of Reiki training to teach students how they can "send" Reiki energy to someone across the room, across the state, and across the world. There are many ways a student can do this and I have tried to list some of my favorite techniques here:

(1). Use your eyes to send Reiki energy to someone, or something. Just stare at the area that is in need of Reiki energy and know that the energy will go there.

(2). Stand in front of the person, or thing, you want to send Reiki energy to. Breathe in Reiki energy and send the energy through your hands to the person or thing you want to send Reiki energy to. Aim the palm of your hands right at them. When using this technique, I like to think of the person being in a big oval (like a cocoon) and I am feeling them and the cocoon up with Reiki energy.

(3). You can write the person's name and personal information on a piece of paper and send, or "beam" Reiki energy right into the piece of paper.

(4) You can use a photograph and "beam" Reiki energy into the photograph.

(5) You can write the person's name and personally information on a piece of paper and place the paper between the palms of your hands and send Reiki energy into the piece of paper.

(6) You can use a proxy, such as a baby doll, and send Reiki energy to the baby doll and intend to go to a specific person.

(7) Light a candle and beam Reiki energy into the candle intending it to go to a specific person.

One thing to remember, it doesn't matter how you decide to send energy to someone, just know that you can do this and affect a change in that person's condition. A typical beaming or long distant healing takes generally 5 to 15 minutes. It very rarely takes longer than that. I have heard of people giving a proxy an hour treatment and "beaming" that treatment to someone far away. I personally have never tried this but I don't see why this wouldn't work. Energy is energy and your intent in all of this is what truly matter anyway.

When using the Beaming technique, some Reiki practitioners imagine the Reiki energy flowing out of their hands like rays from the sun. It is this ray of energy that can be directed to a specific area of the body, a plant, or a pet. Below is a picture of how a Reiki practitioner can send Reiki energy into their own feet.

Diagram #1

Diagram #2

Assignment 1:

  Sit in a comfortable position where you can still see your feet. Now, inhale the Reiki energy and send it to your feet using the Beaming Technique. Send this energy for 5-15 minutes. Report your findings here:

_____

_____

_____

_____

_____

_____

Assignment 2:

Find a willing volunteer and sit 3-6' away from them. Lift your hand sup in front of you with your elbows bent. Have the palms of your hands facing your volunteer. Breathe in the Reiki energy and send this energy to your volunteer through the palms of your hands. Allow the energy to flow for 5-15 minutes. Report your findings here:

_____

_____

_____

_____

_____

_____

Report your volunteer's sensations here:

_____

_____

_____

_____

_____

_____

Try this assignment again, this time only use your eyes. Send the Reiki energy through your eyes to your volunteer. Do this for at least 5 minutes and report your findings here:

_____

_____

_____

_____

_____

_____

Assignment 3:

Find a photograph of someone you would like to send Reiki energy to, or write on a piece of paper the information about someone you would like to send Reiki energy to. Hold this piece of paper in between your hands. Take a deep breath of Reiki energy and send this energy to the paper, or photograph, between your hands. Continue to send this energy continuously for 5-15 minutes. Write down your experiences here:

_____

_____

_____

_____

_____

_____

_____

_____

Assignment 4:

Find yourself a "proxy". This can be a baby doll or a stuffed animal. It doesn't matter so much what you choose to use as the proxy. Now, envision the person you want to send a Reiki healing session to and see that person as the proxy. Begin the Reiki hand positions as you would if the person was there in front of you. Think of the person as you send Reiki energy into the proxy. You can choose between either a quick treatment lasting only 5-15 minute treatment, or a full body treatment lasting up to one hour. It is up to you. Report your findings here:

_____

_____

_____

_____

_____

_____

_____

_____

_____

Gassho

What is Gassho?

Gassho is a form of meditation that Dr. Usui is said to have practiced and taught his students. This is a focused meditation and requires much practice to have enough patience to move through this meditation. Start with only a few minutes at a time and build up to the 20 minutes that is recommended to performing this meditation.

To Do:

Sit down on the floor or in a chair

Close your eyes

Take a slow and deep breath through your nose

Release the breath slowly through your mouth

Repeat the breath in and out

Feel your body begin to relax

Feel your mind begin to relax

Fold your hands together (as if in prayer) in front of you

Focus your attention at the point where your two middle fingers meet

Try to forget everything else

If you begin to think of other things, observe the thought and then let it go

Continue to focus on the point between your two middle fingers

Breathe in and Relax

Exhale out and Let Go.

Assignment:

Every day for the next 21 days you will practice the Gassho meditation. You can spend as little as 5 minutes and as much 30 minutes in this meditation. Report your findings throughout the month. Use extra paper if you need to.

Day 1

Day 2

Day 3

Day 4

Day 5

Day 6

Day 7

Day 8

Day 9

Day 10

Day 11

Day 12

Day 13

Day 14

Day 15

Day 16

Day 17

Day 18

Day 19

Day 20

Day 21

Additional Notes Here:

Chapter Eight

Hand Positioning

How should I hold my Hands?

There are many ways in which you may choose to hold your hands in the Reiki healing session. The old way insisted that both of your hands must be touching each other in each and every hand position. If you wanted to work on both hip positions simultaneously, this would be impossible if you followed this logical pattern. What you would have to do is to use both hands on the left hip, then use both hands on the right hip.

My own belief in this matter is that it isn't important for both hands to ALWAYS be touching each other in the hand positions. The MOST important thing I believe is that your focus and intention be squarely on your client. I would like to talk about some of the ways you can position your hands in a healing session.

Which Hand Position is best for me?

As for which is best to use? This is what I would recommend. I would use Position #1 for Hips, and specific "trouble" spots that the client is having. I would use Position #2 for head, face, and front and back Chakra areas. I would use Position #3 for hand positions for the front and back of the client's body, including the knees and ankles. Then, finally, I would use Position #4 for hand positions of the head, face, elbows, wrists, hands, hips, knees, and ankles.

What are the Major Hand Positioning Called?

There are four major hand positions that are used in a typical Reiki session. They are:

Hands Crossed

Hands Side by Side

Hand over Hand

Hand Sandwiching

Position #1

Hands Crossed

In this position one hand is placed over the area you wish to send Reiki healing energy into, and the other hand is placed directly over the top of the first hand in a crisscross pattern. I don't know if this has anything to do with being left handed or right handed, but when I use this hand positioning, I will place my left hand down on the area first and cover it with my right hand. I am right handed. It may have something more to do with energy connections and flow, but at this writing I haven't investigated this further.

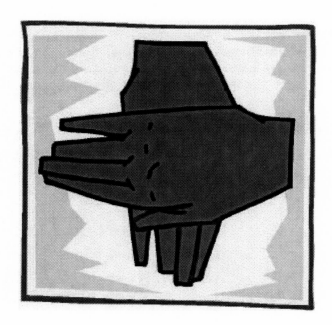

Position #2

Side by Side

This is the standard hand position used during the Reiki healing session. As you can see, both hands are placed together with the sides of the two hands touching each other. Fingers are pointed in the same direction.

Some people believe that where the fingers are pointed are very important when you are working with energy. Very few people want to have the fingers facing upward towards the client's face. There is not much discussion about the good and bad of finger direction, so that the only thing I am going to say to you is to allow your intuition to guide you.

One thing I do in a Reiki healing session is to "sandwich" the client's hand with my own. In this position I am facing the client and my fingers are facing upward towards the client's head. While in this position I am first sending Reiki healing energies into the client and then asking the energy to flow up the client's arm, shoulder, to their head. It is my intention to provide a clear energy channel for the client through that arm. When finished, I do the same thing with the client's other arm. So by doing this I am in a sense directing the flow of the energy with intention.

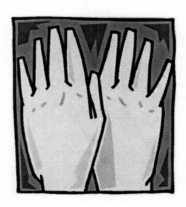

Position #3

Hand over Hand

This is another hand position that is taught to Reiki Level 1 students. In this hand positioning, one hand is placed on the area which is to receive Reiki first, the second hand in then placed on a direct line of the first hand. The fingertips of the first hand are covered with the bottom of the palm of the second hand. In this position, one is able to cover a lot of area in the horizontal pattern.

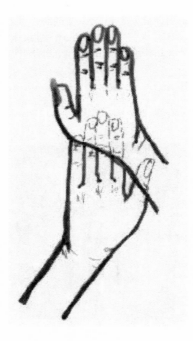

Position #4

Sandwiching

This is the hand position that requires one hand on top of a particular body area as the other hand is under that particular area of the body. This is great hand position for the joints and hands of the body. I use this hand position for the elbows, wrists, hands, hips, knees, ankles, and the feet. It doesn't matter what hand is on top or what hand is underneath. It will all depend on where you are standing in relation to your client. Do whatever is the most comfortable positioning to you. Be aware that you may switch your hands often as you move to different areas of the body. So, just go with the flow!

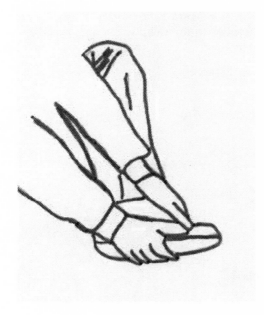

Direction of Hand Placement

Does it matter how I place my hands on the body?

In some circles, it is the belief that the placement of the hand, and in particular the fingers, does matter. In the diagram below are some illustrations to this point. In the first diagram, we see the practitioners hand on the upper back with fingers pointing away from the center of the spine. It is believed that the Reiki practitioner is radiating the Reiki energy to the areas of the body pointing from the center of the upper back area outward.

In the next diagram, the Reiki practitioner has her hands and fingers pointing downward towards the clients' feet. By using the hand position, the Reiki practitioners is sending Reiki energy into the clients' upper back as well as sending it down the spine towards the feet.

You may find yourself in many situations in which your will be more comfortable placing your hands in specific positions. I can honestly say that I have placed my hands in specific hand positions for a particular purpose. The more you practice, the more some of these things will be made known to you. I have found this information very useful in my own practice and I am happy to share it with you here.

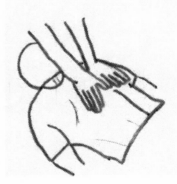

Chapter Nine

Hand Positions for Healing Yourself

Position 1 - The Top of the Head

To Do:

Place both hands gently on the top of your head with palms lying down on your head. Allow the tips of your middle fingers to touch each other. Close your eyes and take a nice, slow, and deep breath in through your nose.

Try to imagine that you are breathing in both oxygen and Reiki energy at the same time. As you breathe in, you allow the energy to enter your body and flow through your body, through your arms, to your hands, out your hands, into your head.

Stay here for 3-5 minutes. This is your Pineal gland. This is where we feel our connectedness to the oneness of the Universe (God, source, Great Spirit, whatever you name for it is).

Position 2 - The Eyes

To Do:

Place both of your hands over your eyes, with palms facing inward towards your eyes. Your fingers should be positioned so that the finger tips of your middle fingers are touching each other.

Alternate Position:

Place both of your hands to cover your entire face with fingers of both hands pointing upwards toward the top of your head. The sides of the hands will be touching.

Note of Caution:

NEVER, EVER, place your hands directly on top of your client's eye. When working on a friend, family member, client, etc. you should place your hands at least 2-4" ABOVE their eyes, never directly on top of their eyes. In some circles, I have seen a tissue placed over someone's' eyes and then the Reiki practitioner would gently place their hands over the clients' eyes. This procedure will totally up to you. I have never placed my hands directly on someone's' eyes, nor do I intend to do so in the future. There is just no need to do this since I believe Reiki energy will reach their eyes even I place my hands several inches above their eyes.

This position is the Pituitary Gland. This position will help those who are suffering from sinus problems, congestion in the head, headaches, eye problems and diseases, mental problems, head problems, nose problems and diseases, fuzzy thinking, the skeletal system, and the nervous system.

Position 3 - The Ears

To Do:

Place the palm of your hands on either side of the jaw and ears with your fingertips pointing towards the back of your head. Close your eyes and take a deep breath imagining both oxygen and Reiki energy entering your body, flowing through your arms, into your hands, out your hands, and into your ears and surrounding area.

Use this area for ear problems and diseases, to reduce stress held in the jaw, TMJ, mouth and tongue problems, gum problems, teeth problems, hearing problems, deafness, ringing in the ear, ear drum damage, and swimmer's ear.

Position 4 - Back of the Head

Or

To Do:

Cup both of your hands and place the heels of your hands under the lower portion of the skull and cradle your head. The fingers of your hands should be extended upwards with the thumbs and index fingers of both hands touching each other. Close your eyes and breathe in the Reiki energy with the oxygen and feel the energy flow through your body, through your arms, through your hands and into the back of your head.

This position will help with people who suffer from headaches and migraines, tension and stress, fuzzy thinking, anxiety, head injuries, and head problems.

Head Position 5 - Throat

 Or

To Do:

Place both of your cupped hands on your throat area with the heels of your hands touching each other. You fingers are pointed towards the back of your neck. Close your eyes and imagine breathing in both oxygen and Reiki energy. Feel the Reiki energy flow through your arms, through your hands and into your neck area.

Use this position for throat problems and diseases, vocal cords, esophagus, mouth problems and diseases, teeth problem and diseases, thyroid, respiratory system, addictions, laryngeal plexus, cervical spine, and parathyroid.

Position 6 - Heart

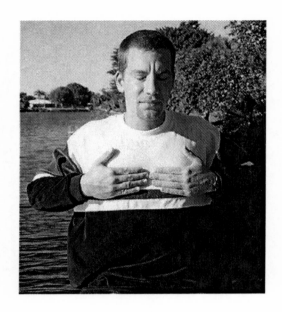

To Do:

Place your hands over your chest area with the fingertips of at least your middle fingers touching, this is nice but is not necessary for the fingers to be touching. When working on a female client, you should NEVER place your hands directly on their breasts. In some states, it is not only immoral; it is illegal to do so. You can place your hands 2-4" above the heart area and send Reiki energy into that area.

This position will help those who are suffering from cardio-vascular problems, arthritis, stroke, hypertension, blood pressure, lung problems and diseases, asthma, allergies, bronchitis pneumonia, AIDS, circulatory system, thymus, heart problems and diseases, blood problems and diseases, gland problems and diseases.

Hand Position 7 - The Solar Plexus

To Do:

Place your hands directly over the Solar Plexus area with your fingertips pointing towards each other. The middle fingers may touch if you wish to.

This position will help those who are suffering from stomach problems and diseases, liver problems and diseases, level of sugar in the blood, Spleen problems and diseases, pancreas problems and diseases, gall bladder problems and diseases, small intestine problems and diseases, assimilation of food in the body, adrenal problems and diseases, solar plexus, and the digestive system.

This is our Seat of Personal Power. Our self motivation stems from this area. Greed, doubt, anger, powerlessness, and guilt all stem from this area.

Position 8 - Spleen

To Do:

Place both of your hands on your Spleen area with the fingertips of your hands facing towards each other, middle fingers touching each other. (Do this if you would like to).

This area will help those who are suffering from Spleen problems and diseases, large intestine problems and diseases, small intestine and diseases, traverse colon problems and diseases, digestive problems and diseases, elimination problems and diseases, constipation, diarrhea, flatulence, womb, urinary problems and diseases, the urinary tract, and problems with the navel.

This area will also people who are suffering from diabetes, infertility, impotence, kidney problems and diseases, muscular system problems, gonads, fallopian tubes, and reproductive problems and diseases.

Position 9 - Base Chakra - Groin Area

To Do:

Place your hands on the base area of your body (where the pubic bone is) with your fingertips pointing downward towards the ground and the thumbs and index fingers touching (if you so desire). Breathe in Reiki energy with the oxygen and feel the Reiki energy flow down through your arms, through your hands and into the groin area.

This position will help those who suffer from groin pulls, groin problems and diseases, illium muscle, and sexual problems and diseases.

Hand Position 10 - Base - The Hips

To Do:

Place your right hand on your right hip and your left hand on your left hip with fingertips pointing towards the front of your body and slowly downward. Close your eyes and breathe in oxygen mixed with Reiki energy. Feel the Reiki energy flow down your arms; flow through your hands and into your hips and hip area.

This position will help those who are suffering from hip problems and diseases, ovarian cancer, problems and diseases of the ovaries and gonads, sexual problems and diseases, leg problems and diseases, obesity, bone disorders, constipation, hemorrhoids, diarrhea, and sciatica.

Hand Position 11 - Back of Neck

To Do:

Place both of your hands on the back of your neck with fingers facing downward. You can have the fingers touching if you so desire. Breathe in Reiki energy and feel it flow through your arms, through your hands and into the back of your neck.

Use this position to help people who are suffering from neck problems and diseases, headaches, circulation problems, muscular problems and diseases, fevers, thyroid problems, vocal chords, esophagus problems, and respiratory system.

Hand Position 12 - Adrenals

To Do:

Place your hands on your back as high up as you can comfortably reach them. The fingertips of your hands should be pointing in towards each other. If this position is too uncomfortable for you, then you can skip this hand position. Breathe in oxygen mixed with Reiki energy and feel the Reiki energy flowing through your body, down your arms, through your hands and into your adrenals and the adrenal area.

This hand position will help those who are suffering from adrenal problems and diseases including low energy and low metabolism.

Hand Position 13 - Lower Back

To Do:

Place both of your hands on your lower back with the fingertips of your hands pointing inward towards the middle of your spine. It is not necessary for the fingertips of your hands to be touching. Breathe in the Reiki energy and feel it flow down your arms, through your hands and into the lower back area.

This hand position will help those people who are suffering from lower back problems and diseases, disc problems and diseases, spine problems and diseases, sciatica, digestive problems and diseases, intestinal problems and diseases, constipation, diarrhea, elimination problems and diseases, kidney problems and diseases, skeletal system, elimination system, urinary problems and diseases, reproductive problems and diseases, poor circulation and obesity.

Hand Position - 14 - Tailbone

To Do:

Place your hands over the center line of your spine with the fingertips of your hands pointing downward. It is not necessary to have your fingers touching.

This hand position will help those who are suffering from back problems and diseases, sciatica, disk problems and diseases, kidney problems and diseases, leg problems and diseases, poor circulation, skeletal system, constipation, diarrhea, elimination problems and diseases, urinary problems and diseases, varicose veins, hemorrhoids, bone disorders, and frequent illnesses.

Hand Position 15 - Knees

To Do:

Place the palm of your right hand on your right knee and the palm of your left hand on your left knee. Have the fingertips of both of your hands pointing downward. Breathe in the Reiki energy and feel the energy flow down through your arms, flow through your hands and into the knee and knee area of your body.

This position will help those who are suffering from knee problems and diseases, leg problems and diseases, sciatica, poor circulation, varicose veins, and problems of the skeletal system. The knee is also associated with the digestive system.

Hand Position 16 - The Ankle

To Do:

Place your right hand on your right ankle and your left hand on your left ankle. Breathe in Reiki energy and feel the energy flow down through your arms, flow through your hands and into your ankles.

This hand position will help those who are suffering from ankle problems and diseases, feet problems and diseases, leg problems and diseases, poor circulation, sciatica, varicose veins, bone disorders, and the skeletal system.

Hand Position #17 - The Foot

To Do:

In this position we are using the technique called "sandwiching". This is where both of our hands are surrounding a particular area of the client's body. The Sandwiching hand position works wonderful on joint areas such as the elbows, wrists, knees and ankles. I also use it for the hands and feet. This position will help those who suffer from feet problems, varicose veins, circulation problems, and skeletal problems.

Chapter 10

Mudras

There are Three Major Mudras that are associated with the Reiki System of Natural Healing. You do NOT have to be able to do any of these in order to practice Reiki. In face, most of the Western lineages do not include any of these Mudras in their teaching, nor in their books and manuals. They are listed here because Mudras are very common in Chinese, Japanese, and Eastern Cultures. It is said that Dr. Usui himself used Mudras before, during and after Reiki sessions. I have enjoyed using them myself and have found them worth learning. The rest is up to you.

Mudra 1 - Sha

Sha

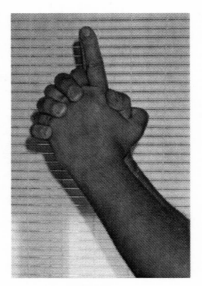

To Do:

Begin by interlacing all your fingers together. Now, extend the index fingers of both hands and press them together. This Mudra is called SHA. This Mudra is used for Spiritual healing and to bring the spiritual light into your healing sessions. This Mudra is the one most often associated with the Reiki "Dai Ko Mio" Power Symbol. It was taught that the SHA Mudra should be practiced by Reiki practitioners before any type of Reiki healing session is performed.

The extended fingers are used to gather up the energy that is within the body and direct that energy, through the fingers, in a focused thought to affect the healing of a particular area of the body.

This Mudra can also be used to break through any "barriers" that may be forming a wall that is used to block healing. If this is the case, you can use your fingers to gather up the energy and then "blast" through those barriers and walls that keep one from healing.

To use this Mudra, keep your eyes closed for 30 seconds while you keep your focus on the Reiki point that lies about 2" below the navel. In martial arts, this area is known as the Tan Ten, or seat of balance. This Mudra will help to bring in spiritual energy that will enable the Reiki practitioners to begin the Reiki treatment using proper hand positions.

It is also very powerful to say a Mantra when using a Mudra. There is a specific mantra associated with each and every Mudra that you use. The mantra that is used when the mudra SHA is performed is the following:

On Ha Ya Bai Shira Ma Ta Ya So Wa Ka

Mudra 2 - RIN

Rin

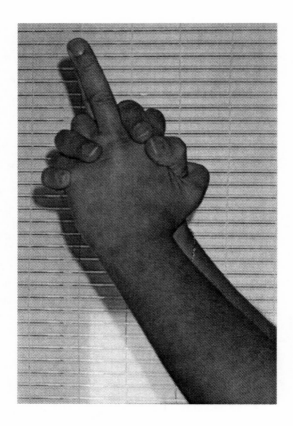

To Do:

Begin by interlacing your fingers together. Now, extend the middle fingers of both of your hands and place them together. This Mudra is called RIN.

The RIN Mudra is associated with the Reiki symbol, "Cho Ku Rei". You can use this Mudra when you need additional Power, Strength of Mind, and Strength of Body. Use this Mudra whenever you need physical, mental, and/or emotional, strength. The RIN Mudra represents the Power of God. It can destroy ignorance and create inner peace, power, and wisdom.

To use this Mudra, you begin by focusing your energy and attention on the point where you feel the pulse between your middle fingers. Hold this position until you can feel your hands ready to be put down on your client.

To use this Mudra, begin by keeping your eyes closed and allow spirit to come in closer to you. Envision the center of the Reiki point located about 2" below the navel being filled with radiant white light. Hold this position until the hands feel ready to lie down on the client.

The mantra associated with this Mudra is:

On Bai Shira Man To Ya So Was Ka

Mudra 3 - Kai

Kai

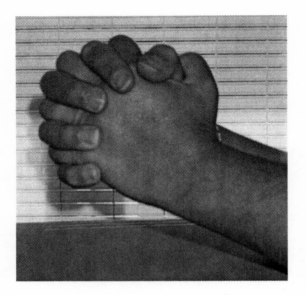

To Do:

Begin by interlacing all your fingers together and pressing the palms together. This is the Mudra, KAI. This Mudra is used to help clear your mind and to still your thoughts. When performed correctly, you will be able to sense all that surrounds you, including the ability to sense danger.

Using Kai will enable you to feel the emotions of others. You will know how someone will react in a given situation. You will have insight into many things, including the ability to see the outcome of your actions before you do them, enabling you to affect them.

Kai is also used to break the bonds of passions and desires. I believe this is in the context where the passions and/or dressers would affect your higher state of being. Examples of that would be overeating, smoking, drinking, etc. If the urge of these desires cloud your mind, then you cannot achieve the state of knowingness that is your birthright.

You can use this Mudra during a healing session when you need more information on the client you are working on. You can also use this Mudra when you need to know the true cause of an affliction. To do this, you will sit in a quiet meditative state using this Mudra and just ask your question. You will then wait for an answer. Answers do come quickly. Don't try to second guess the answers that you receive and don't try to ask for further, minor details. Accuracy will come with practice.

Using Mudras:

The most common way to use a Mudra is to sit with it in quiet contemplation and meditation. If you have any questions to ask, you can do the following exercise:

Exercise:

Prepare yourself and your focus. Ask the question, and sit with the Mudra, Kai. Connect yourself to the Source (or whatever name you call it). You will now wait to receive your answer. Go ahead and practice this on yourself, your partner, or a volunteer.

_____

_____

_____

_____

_____

_____

_____

_____

If you are faced with a client who has had a chronic problem with a particular part of their body (say their foot) you can use the Kai Mudra to discover what the problem is. You would just fold your hands in the Kai position over their foot and ask the question and wait for the answer.

Using Mudras in this way can be very efficient and helpful. You can use the Kai Mudra on other parts of the body to which energy does not seem to flow smoothly. Be patient with yourself if you do not receive answers to your questions. With practice, you will be able to hear your answers very quickly. Most people get so discouraged with themselves that they quit trying all together. Don't let this happen to you. Just as you had to have training wheels on you first "big" bicycle, so too will you have to wait until you are ready to listen to your intuition.

Chapter Eleven

Hand Positions for Healing Others

Hand Positions for the Front of the Body

Position One - Crown of Head

With client lying face up, sit (or stand) behind the client and place both of your hands on the client head. In the picture above, I am placing my hands with thumbs touching and fingers pointing upwards. I am sending Reiki energy into the client's head first and then, through my intention, I am sending Reiki energy down through the head to the client's body.

As an added benefit while sending Reiki energy, I am adding positive and loving thoughts as well. I send thoughts such as love, peace, harmony, and stillness. I do this with clients who I am familiar with what is going on in their life. This little addition to the hand position really works wonders on my clients.

Use this position for imbalances in the head due to headaches and head injuries. This position will help with stress. Use this position for the pineal and hypothalamus gland. This position will help to improve motor (and thinking) functions.

Position Two - Face/Brow Chakra

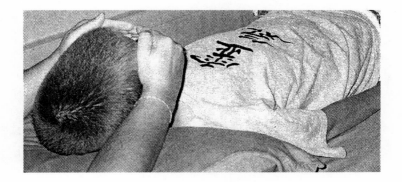

      Have the client lay face up on a massage table while you stand, or sit, at the client's head. Place both of your hands over the face area of your client. Be sure to cover the client's eyes as well as well as their nose with the hand position. Place both of your hands, thumbs touching and fingers pointing towards the client's toes. DO NOT under any circumstance; lay your hands directly on your client's face. Position your hands to about 2-4" above the client's face and hold them there for the entire time.

      If you have difficulty holding your hands extended above the body for any amount of time there is an option for you. You may place a folded tissue over your client's eyes and then proceed to place your hands gently on the tissue.

      This hand position will help with imbalances of the Thalamus and pituitary glands. Eye problems, headaches, sinus problems, allergies, hay fever, and mouth, gum, and teeth problems will be helped with this position.

Position Three - Ears

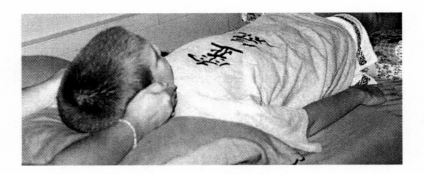

Have your client lie face up on the massage table as you sit, or stand, behind the client's head. Place both of your hands on either side of the clients' ear area. Your right hand should be on the client's right ear and your left hand should be on your client's left ear. Once again, it is my suggestion that you DO NOT place your hand directly on your client's ear, but rather leave your hands 2-4" away from their ears. If this is a difficult position for you, you may try to rest your arms on the pillow underneath your client's head for additional support.

This hand position will help with all hearing and ear problems. This position includes headaches and all mouth, teeth, jaw and gum problems including TMJ.

Position Four - Throat

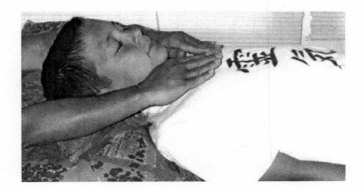

Have you client lie on a massage table while you sit or stand behind the client's head. Place both of your hands over your client's throat area. I generally have my thumbs or first fingers touching each other with all the other fingers pointed inward and downward towards the client's toes. Again, I do not lay my hands directly on the client's throat area but place my hands 2-4" above the client's body.

Placing your hands directly on the client's throat can make it highly uncomfortable for the client and cause a gagging reflex, something I am sure you would prefer to avoid. Also this is a very emotional area for most people and placing your hands directly on the throat may cause many negative emotional responses.

This hand position will help with imbalances of the immune system and metabolism. All throat problems are helped with this position. Also included in this hand position is: calcium absorption, weight control, and energy stimulator.

Position Five - Heart

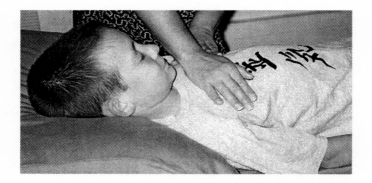

Have you client lie face up on a massage table while you stand or sit to one side of your client. At this point, it does not matter if you stand or sit to the right of the client or to the left. In some energy systems there is preference but not for the Reiki system of natural healing.

You may choose which of the hand positioning you would like to do now. These hand positioning choices were listed earlier on in this book. You may refer back to it now if you need to. I personally place one hand on the heart area and place the other hand further over the same area with the heel of that hand barely covering my first hand. You will be able to cover a lot of area with this hand position.

If you are working on a female client, DO NOT place your hands directly on her chest. In most states this is illegal! Be considerate of the client's feelings and vulnerability. You should have your hands positioned 2-4" above the breast area. Another option is to use the crisscross hands and place them directly over the Heart Chakra area without touching the breasts at all. You will have to decide how best to approach this situation for yourself.

This hand position helps imbalances in the lymph system, the ovaries/cycle of a woman, tumors, cysts, headaches, breast problems including lactation, and PMS.

Position Six - Solar Plexus

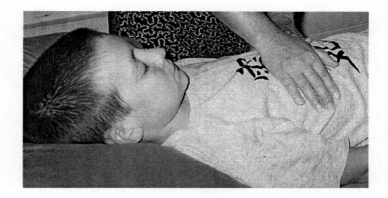

Have your client lie face up on a massage table while you sit or stand next to the client. It does not matter which side you choose to stand, but be consistent. If you choose to stand on the left side of the client, then continue on with the hand positions while standing on the left side. Do NOT continue to switch back and forth with each hand position. Think of the nice uninterrupted flow of energy.

Place your hands just as you did in the prior position. This position is located beginning at the base of the rib cage and above the navel. You can place your hands directly on this area if you choose to and you may decide on which hand position to use.

Use this hand position for all digestive and stomach problems. This position will help imbalances in blood sugar levels (such as diabetes). Spleen, liver, gall bladder, and the pancreas will all be helped with this position. Constipation problems will also be helped with this area.

Position Seven - Spleen

    Have your client lie on a massage table while you stand or sit next to your client. Place both of your hands on the sacral area located just below the navel. Choose the hand positioning you want and place your hands on the area.

    This hand position will help with imbalances in the menstrual cycle. This position will also help the bladder, infections, arthritis, migraines and headaches, ovaries, cysts, lower intestines, colon, the adrenal and pineal glands, and all vaginal or uterus disorders.

Position Eight - Base Chakra

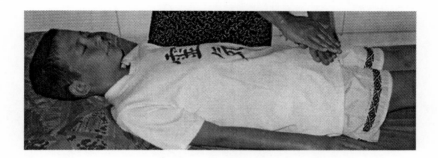

Have your client lie on a massage table while you stand to the side. Place one hand 1-6" above the pubic area and place the other hand on top of the first hand-NO NOT TOUCH THE PUBIC AREA!).

This hand position will help with problems such as Impotence, varicose veins, poor circulation, sciatica, cystitis, herpes, prostate (in men), leg injuries and problems, hemorrhoids, knee and ankle problems, and problems of the feet.

Position Nine - Knees

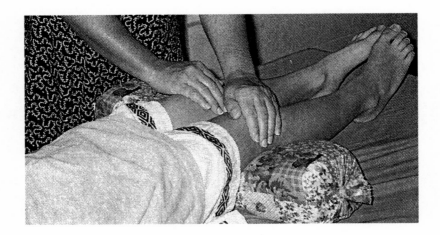

Have your client lie face up while you stand or sit to their side. Place your hands very gently on your client's knees. It is very important for you to know that if you add any pressure to your hands while in this position you could injure your client by hyper extending their knees. So please, just place your hands (with no weight to them) on the knee area. If you are not sure how strong your touch is, then you may wish to place you hands just above the knee area, above the kneecap.

Use this position to help all knee, leg, ankle, and foot problems including sciatica and varicose veins. This position will also help with blood circulation.

Position Ten - Ankles

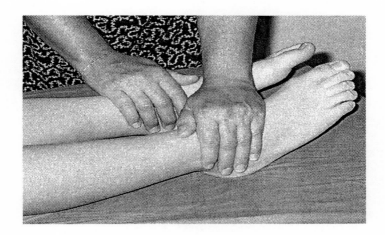

Have your client lie on a massage table as you stand or sit to their side. Place both of your hands gently on your client's ankles. It doesn't matter which hand you place on which ankle, just place your hands where it is comfortable for you. This position can also be done while you are sitting or standing at the feet of your client. So try both positions and see what is best suited for you.

This position will help with all ankles and feet problems including swollen ankles and varicose veins. Use this position for circulation problems, anterior tibia's problems, and shin splints.

Position Eleven - Feet

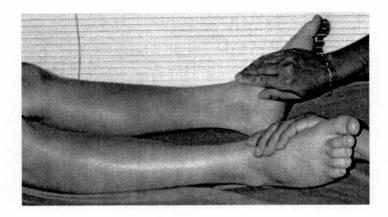

Have your client lie on a massage table while you sit or stand at their feet. Place both of your hands on the inside of your client's feet. Your left hand should be on your client's left foot and your right hand should be on your client's right foot.

Use this position for all foot problems including corns. Other conditions helped by this hand position are; stress, circulatory problems, and spaciness.

Position Twelve - Bottom of Feet

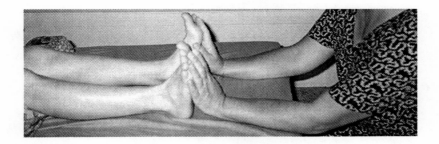

Have your client lie on a massage table while you sit or stand at their feet. Place you right hand on the bottom of your client's right foot with your fingers pointing upwards toward your client's toes. Place your left hand on the bottom of you client's left foot with your fingers pointing upwards toward your client's toes.

In this position I first send Reiki healing energy into the client's foot, then I imagine the energy flowing up the client's leg, up the torso, up the shoulders, up the neck, and up through and out of the head. I see the energy being accepted by the client's body and pushing all illnesses and dis-harmony out.

I use this hand position to help remove negative energies, as well as, other toxins from the client's body.

Hand Positions for the Back of the Body

Position Thirteen - Back of Head

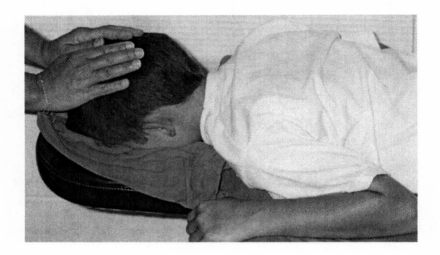

Have your client lie face down on a massage table (preferably in a face cradle). You will stand (or sit) at the head of your client and gently place both of your hands, with thumbs slightly touching, on the back of your client's head. The entire palm of your hand will be on your client's hand with your fingers pointing down towards your client's toe.

Use this hand position for imbalances in the Pineal and Hypothalamus gland. This hand position will also help people who are suffering from headaches and head injuries, stroke, eye problems, nose bleeds, and other eye and nose problems.

Position Fourteen - Back of Neck

Have your client lying face down on the massage table with their face in a face cradle. Stand, or sit, to the side of your client and place both hands on the bottom of the neck (upper back area). Please, DO NOT put your hands directly on the back of the neck vertebra. You can cause injury if you apply pressure here. Your hands should be positioned on the upper back area where the shoulders meet. You can choose the hand positions you like the best here. I prefer the hand over hand position for this area of the body.

Use this hand position for client's who suffer from throat problems, stress and tension, spinal problems and headaches.

Position Fifteen - Back of Heart Chakra

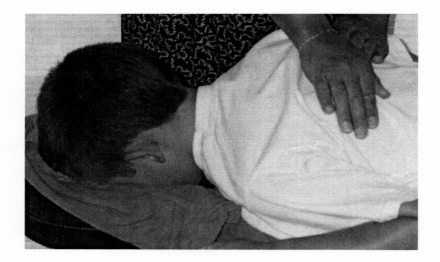

Have your client lying face down on a massage table with their face in a face cradle. You will stand or sit to the side of your client. Place your hand directly over the Heart area which is located between the lower scapula area, and center of rib cage. You may choose the hand position you would like to use. For this position, I generally use the hand over hand position.

Use this hand position to treat all Heart and Lung problems. This position will also help client's who are suffering from stress and tension, nervousness, spinal problems, and all emotional issues of love and acceptance.

Position Sixteen - Back of Solar Plexus Chakra

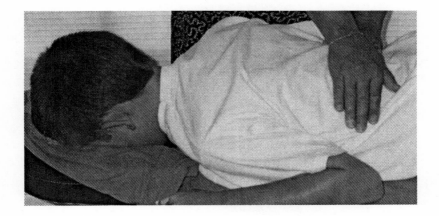

Have your client lying face down on the massage table with their face in the face cradle. You will stand or sit to the side of your client and place both of your hands on their Solar Plexus area. This area is located right over the adrenals, just below the ribcage but above the navel. You may use the hand position you feel most comfortable with. I usually use the hand over hand position for this area.

This hand position will help those client's who suffer from imbalances in the blood system such as diabetes, hypoglycemia, and hyperglycemia. Migraines, stress, tension, male reproductive problems, infections, and female reproductive problems are all helped with this hand positioning.

Position Seventeen - Back of Spleen Chakra

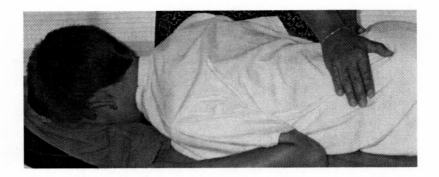

Have your client lying on a massage table face down with their face in a face cradle. You will stand to the side of your client and place both of your hands on the client's spleen area. This area is located at the waistline area where the kidneys are located, around the navel area. You may choose the hand positions you feel most comfortable with or are guided to use for this area. For me, I generally use the hand over hand positioning.

This hand position will help client's who suffer from kidney problems, spleen, edema, infections, high blood pressure, and arthritis.

Position Eighteen - Back of Base Chakra

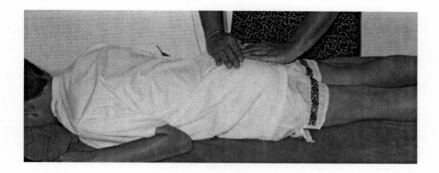

Have your client lying face down on a massage table with their face in a face cradle. You will stand or sit to the side of your client and place both of your hands over the coccyx area. The coccyx area is located at the base of the spine, the tailbone. You may choose to use whatever hand position you are comfortable with in this position. The above picture shows the zigzag hand position being used. I generally use the hand over hand position for this position.

This position will help client's who suffer from intestinal disorders, lower back problems, lumbar problems and disorders, and sacral disorders. This also includes sciatic problems.

Position 19 - Back of Knees

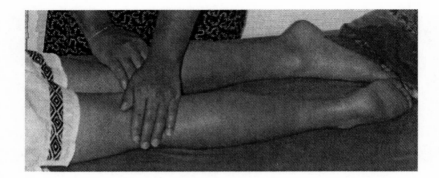

Have your client lying on a massage table face down with their face in a face cradle. You will stand or sit to the side of your client and place both of your hands gently on the backs of their knees. Place one hand on one knee, and the other hand on the other knee. It does not matter which hand you choose to place on which knee, as long as the position is comfortable for you.

A word of caution here: Please, Please, Please, while in this position, do NOT under any circumstances add pressure to your hands. You can invoke injury on your client should you do so. Some practitioners who get tired towards the end of the session may use their hands to help hold them up. I would rather see you end a session before you do that.

Use this hand position to help client's who suffer from Sciatic nerve problems, varicose veins, circulation in the legs, and knee injuries.

Position 20 - Back of Ankles

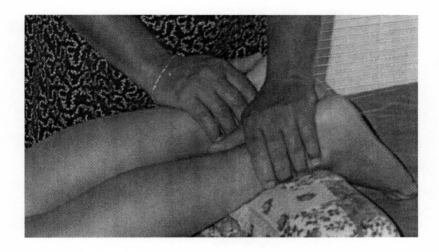

   Have client lying on a massage table face down with their face in the face cradle. You will stand or sit to the client's side or you may choose to stand at the client's feet for this hand position. You will place both of your hands on the client's ankles. You will place one hand on one of the ankles, and the other hand on the other ankle. It does not matter which hand you choose to place on which ankle, as long as it is comfortable to you.

   This hand position will help client's who suffer from sciatic nerve problems, circulation in the legs and feet, varicose veins, edema, and ankles problems.

Position 21 - Bottoms of Feet

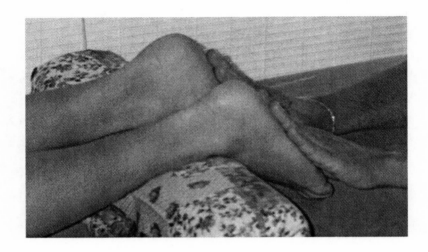

Have your client lying face down on a massage table with their face in a face cradle. You will stand or sit at your client's feet. You will place both of your hands on your client's feet, one hand on the bottom of one foot and the other hand on the bottom of the other foot. It just makes common sense in this position that your left hand will be place on your client's left foot and your hand will be placed on your client's right foot. I usually sit for this one as I tend to send energy while in this position.

As an added note: Be sure your own feet are planted solidly on the ground. Be sure you are grounded. I use this hand position for a three-fold mission.

1.) I send energy into the soles of the feet. In Reflexology, it is believed that all of your organs and body systems can be located on the soles of your feet. Sending Reiki energy into the bottoms of your feet just makes good sense.

2.) I use this hand position to "push" Reiki energy up through the legs and out of the client's crown Chakra (top of head) to help remove any additional blockages of energy that is in the body.

3) Then I pull the energy down from the client's crown Chakra (top of head), down their body, down their legs, and into their feet. I then draw that energy through my own hands, through my body, and down into my feet where I send it into the Earth. (I send it into the Earth with the intention of it being transmuted into Love.)

This hand position will help client's who are suffering from sciatic nerve problems, circulation in the legs and feet, varicose veins, feet problems, and grounding issues and blockages.

Chapter Twelve

Closing the Session

Methods and Techniques

There are many ways in which Reiki practitioners may choose to close their Reiki sessions. Below is a list of some commonly used ways to "close" the session:

Angel Wings

In performing the angel wings closing technique, you will stand facing your client on either side of the massage table. Your client will have their face down in the face cradle during this time. You will begin by placing both of your hands on the upper back of your client. You will then do a wide sweeping motion to the outside of the client (towards the clients shoulder) and then sweep your hands down to the clients' lower spine. You are imitating the "wings of an angel". When you reach the lower spine, you will lift your hands off the client's body and place them once again at the to of the client's back and sweep your hands down the client's body to the lower spine, lift your hands off the body and repeat one more time. This is done a total of three complete sweeps.

One special note here is this; you should do this exercise with caution. Don't be rough. You are just gently and lovingly sweeping your hands over the client's body. Some people will barely feel the movement because you are doing this so gently. If you do not want to (or can't) touch the person's body, then this whole exercise may be down 2-4" above the client's body. It is a nice finishing touch either way.

The Cocoon

The cocoon is something I teach all of my Reiki level 1 students. While working on a client's energy field, you have probably opened up their Chakra systems. You should never allow your client's to leave you with their Chakra systems opened like that. So, this is one technique I use to close down each and every Chakra before the client leaves the treatment room.

When finished with the session, you will take both of your hands and imagine circling your client and placing them into a large cocoon. I do a sweeping motion with my arms around the client as I stand off to the side of the table. I do the sweeping motion a total of three times. When finished, I visualize the client in a safe and loving cocoon and I fill that cocoon with Reiki energy. I will then tap them on their shoulder (to signify the session is over) and say "Thank You".

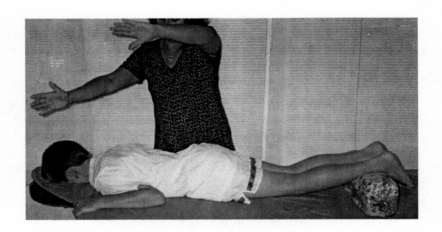

The Spinal Zigzag

I use this technique on clients who I know will be driving right after the healing session. Some client's are so relaxed during a Reiki treatment that they have fallen asleep. The last thing I want to see is the client behind the wheel of a car! For those clients who must drive home immediately following a session, I do this technique:

You will place the index finger and middle finger of either hand on the OUTSIDE of the client's spine. You will in NO time actually touch the client's spine. You can do severe damage to the client should you press on the spine. With your two fingers on the outside of the spine, you will zigzag your fingers down the spine to the bottom of the spine, lift your fingers up off the body, return them to the top of the spine, and repeat the zigzag motion down the spine, lift the fingers off the body, return them to the top of the spine, and repeat motion one more time. I do this method for a total of three complete motions. I them touch the client's shoulder (to signify the end of the session) and say Thank-You.

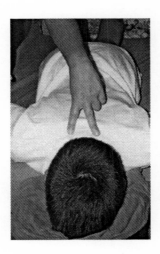

Which way is Best for Me?

There is no right way or wrong way to perform a closing session. In a lot of cases, I use ALL of the techniques listed here in additional to several others that we will discuss in later books and manuals. For now, it is just important that you realize that you must do something to finish the Reiki session and close the auric field of your client before they leave your room. What you choose to do is up to you. You can use many combinations of a dozen or so techniques. The choice is yours, just do something!

Hygienic Concerns for the Practitioner

Are there Hygienic Concerns for Reiki Practitioners?

Yes. It is a common belief by many Reiki practitioners and students that Reiki is a hands-on healing technique. Well, yes and no. The human touch is a valuable and loving modality, but there are times when touching another person are impossible. Reiki can work not only on the physical body of a person, but in the auric field of that person also.

It is highly advised that all Reiki practitioners adopt some common sense and hygienic practices to their healing sessions. First, get into the habit of washing your hands before and after each treatment. This cleansing procedure will have a double benefit. In the field of energy, external forces can affect the energetic field. Washing your hands before a session not only is proper hygiene, it also acts as a cleansing of the practitioners own energy field. This assures that the client will receive not only clean, washed hands, but hands that are also free of the energetic "junk" of the practitioners. This holds doubly true for washing hands after a treatment where the practitioner will not want to take on their clients' physical dis-ease nor their "junk" energy.

Secondly, change the sheets and wash them after each session. Some practitioners actually believe that because their clients are fully dressed for a session that they do not have to strip the sheets and wash them between clients. This is both unpleasant and unsanitary. Would you want to lie on sheets that have been used by not one, but several people before you? Of course not, so why would you subject someone else to that. It is not only the physical body that I am concerned about but also the energetic body. Would you want to lay in someone else's cast of energies? I know I sure wouldn't. Be sure to wipe down your massage table as well as the sheets after each session. A good disinfectant would be fine, or you can purchase a spray specifically formulated and designed for massage therapist by ordering online or visiting your local alternative health care store. Take the time necessary to supply your clients with a safe and healthy environment for their healing sessions.

Thirdly, if your client has any burns, open sores, blisters, cuts, etc. DO NOT put your hands on those areas of the body. You can work just as effectively and safely a few inches above the area in question.

In most states, expect a visit from a state health inspector hi will ensure that proper procedures are followed. Every state requirement is different but most follow the same general rules and regulations for their massage therapist as they do for Reiki practitioners. So, before setting up your practice, check with your own State on your local requirements to practice Reiki in your area.

Legal Issues Concerning the Practitioners

Are there legal issues with practicing Reiki?

Yes. Whenever one person "lays" or "places" their hand on another person's body, a potential for harm exists. It is this concept that has many regulating bodies up in arms and with good reason. How can you regulate Reiki practitioners? How can you give Reiki practitioners one set of rules for all of them to follow? How can you insure that all Reiki practitioners are taught proper hygiene techniques? Well, because of this and other reasons, many States have taken it upon themselves to find a way to regulate the practice of Reiki.

Each Reiki practitioner comes into the field of Reiki energy work with their own set of values and healing arts. Some practitioners use only Reiki in their sessions while other practitioners use Reiki as an adjunct to other forms of healing. The client (the public at large) does not really know if what they are receiving is truly Reiki, or some sort of other treatment to which Reiki has been added. There are no true guidelines on this subject to date.

Some states now require that a Reiki practitioner must be a licensed massage therapist or a licensed and practicing medical doctor. To be sure of the requirements in your own particular state, you must call and ask your own licensing boards. Never assume because so and so down the street is practicing Reiki without a license that it is all right for you to do the same. It may not be. If you are caught practicing without a license you can be fined, or worse. So be sure to find out your legal standing first before you hang out your shingle. Also consider local ordinances. While it may be legal for you to practice Reiki in your state without a license, it may not be legal to practice it your own home. So, be sure to check with State AND local licensing bureaus.

Then again is the issue of insurance. Whenever you are involved with the public, there is a question of risk and the possibility of being sued. What if the person claims you caused them severe damage? What if the client falls off your massage table and breaks their hip? What if they sue you?

Some practitioners believe that if they give their services away for free that they cannot be sued. I hate to burst your bubble, but you can be sued. If you own something that can be taken away from you in a lawsuit (home, car, and other valuables), then you should sincerely consider carrying insurance on yourself. Yes, there are companies out there who insure Reiki practitioners. If you are a massage therapist, or other licensed health care practitioner, then you probably are already carrying insurance on yourself, but you should check and be sure that Reiki will be covered under your current policy. Don't expect someone else to do this for you; this is your responsibility, so take care of it now!

On the issue of applying for a reverend license and sliding through the system's loopholes, think again. Many people believe that the law stating there is a separation of church and state means that they can practice Reiki under the guise of spiritual healing and not get a license. In most states this is legal but it still doesn't release you from being sued. If you choose to go this route, I would highly recommend talking with your lawyer and insurance agent before committing to practicing this, or any other, form of natural healing.

Please, never manipulate (massage) your client without proper certifications, training, and licenses. If you are not experienced, you can cause great damage to your client. Leave massages to the licensed massage therapist.

Ethical Issues for the Practitioner

What are the Ethical Issues concerning practicing Reiki?

Now that you are a Reiki practitioner, you want to go around and heal everyone and everything in your path. You, your family members, friends, neighbors, and co workers all become easy targets for you to practice your new gift of Reiki on. So, what is stopping you? Here comes the ethical issue of pushing your belief system (using Reiki) on another person without their permission. I have seen some practitioners give their spouses Reiki while they were sleeping because they had refused treatment when they were awake. This is wrong, wrong, wrong. You want other people to do this to you so why would you force yourself on other people? Where is the respect in each person own integrity?

Can you treat someone who has told you "No"? The better question is "What gives you the right to decide for that person what is right and best for them?" It is my own firm belief that you should never, ever, treat someone who has clearly told you that they did not want to receive a Reiki treatment. It is their right and their own free will to decide for themselves what it is that they want and do not want in their own life - not yours!

As a Reiki practitioner you must learn to respect other people's rights as you would like them to respect you and how you have chosen to live your own life. Just because you love someone does not give you the right to chose for them either. There are other things you can do to help. A friend of mine had her father going in for surgery and asked me to send him Reiki energy. Since I could not ask him in person, I sat in silence and asked my higher self if I could send him this Reiki energy. I received a loud and clear "NO". I respected his wishes and sent the Reiki energy to my friend and her mother as I could see them sitting in the waiting room, I sent the Reiki energy to the surgeon who was performing the surgery, and I even sent the Reiki energy to the nurses and other staff members who were in attendance at the surgery. This did not take away the patients right not to receive Reiki energy.

Another story was from a distraught mother of a young teenage girl. She and her daughter had spent several days yelling and arguing without any clear developments. The mother wanted to give her daughter Reiki but the daughter refused. What was the mother to do? I suggested to the mother to respect her daughter's right to refuse the Reiki energy, but that there was a way she could help the situation. Since the mother still owned the house in which they lived, and the daughter was still a minor, I had the mother Reiki the daughter's room and her belongings while she was at school. After only one day of sending loving energy into the daughter's room, the mother called me the following day to tell me of the miracle that had occurred. She and her daughter were back together again and happy.

What about sending Reiki long distance? If you cannot ask the person for a verbal "yes" or "no", then you can close your eyes and sit quietly. Take a deep breath and ask the question,

"Can I send Reiki energy to _____"?

Wait for an answer. You should receive the answer very quickly; it will be the first thing that pops in your head. Don't diagnose it or pick at it, the answer is what it is - just accept it. Don't second guess yourself.

Remember the earth, the water, the animals, and the tree. These all accept Reiki energy openly and freely every day. Share some of the gift of Reiki energy with them. Don't forget to give yourself daily Reiki treatment and share with your family and friends as often as you can.

Reiki Blessings

The Symbol for Reiki

The Ancient Form

Pictured below is the ancient form of the symbol, Reiki. This is called the Kanji style. It is from the ancient times of the Japanese language. There still exists today many dialects in Japan. Each dialect has its own symbols and meaning. Some are the same (universal) while others are quite closed to their own region. In the Japanese language, there is no "R" sound. When Dr. Usui started to use Reiki in Japan, he did not call it Reiki (ray-key). In fact, he did not call it anything. It wasn't until his death that his remaining students came together to form the "Reiki system of natural healing". In Japan, Reiki is not pronounced (ray-key). Instead, it is called, (lay-key). The "R" sound in Japan is actually an "L" sound.

In this ancient form of symbol, there is a lot more information that is given. Each line and stroke is a meaning unto itself. The putting together of many lines and strokes make up the story, or the information, that is the symbol. Much meaning has been lost to the present day world of the total meaning of this Kanji symbol since its dialect is no longer practiced in Japan.

The Modern Form

In this modern form of the Reiki symbol, we clearly see two separate and unique symbols together. The top symbol is "Rei" and the bottom symbol should be more familiar to us as "Ki". The Rei symbol has many definitions and meanings. Among them are the following information connected to the Reiki symbol: Universal, Spirit, Ghost, Supernatural, and Consciousness of spirit.

The Ki symbol is called many things around the world. In China this Ki is called Chi, or Qi. In Sanskrit and India, this Ki is called Prana. In the Native American language, Ki would be called the Great Spirit. Whatever it is called, Ki means life force energy. Ki is the energy of life that surrounds every living thing. The Chinese uses this knowledge of life force energy in their practice of acupuncture.

It is our contention here that Reiki affects the energy of the person you are working on. When a client's Ki, or energy life force, is low, they are more prone to illnesses. Giving a client Reiki can help enhance their immune system and restore their weakened "Ki".

Client In-Take Form

(Please Print)

Date _____

Name _____

Address _____

City, State, and Zip Code

_____

Telephone Number

_____

Email Address _____

Who to Call in Case of Emergency

_____

Relationship

_____

Write here all current problems

_____

_____

_____

_____

_____

Write here all medications you are currently taking

_____

_____

_____

_____

_____

_____

_____

Is this your first Reiki Session? _____

What are you hoping to achieve through this Reiki Session?

_____

_____

_____

_____

_____

Name of your primary health care physician

_____

Practitioner Notes:

Mrs. Takata's Master Students

Before her death, Mrs. Takata was able to initiate twenty-two Reiki Masters. Listed below is that list of Reiki masters that she initiated before her passing The names are listed in alphabetical order:

George Araki

Dorothy Baba

Ursula Baylow

Rick Bockner

Barbara Brown

Fran Brown

Patricia Ewing

Phyllis Lei Furumoto (Takata's granddaughter)

Beth Gray

John Gray

Iris Ishikura

Harry Kuboi

Ethel Lombardi

Barbara McCullough

Mary McFadyen

Paul Mitchell

Bethel Phaigh

Barbara Weber Ray

Shinobu Saito

Virginia Samdahl

Wanja Twan

Hawayo Takata's Sister

Additional Reading List

Reiki, the Healing Touch, First and Second Degree Manual by William Lee Rand, 1991

The Reiki Touch by J.C. Stewart, 1989

The Complete Reiki Handbook by W. Lubeck, 1994

Empowerment through Reiki by P. Horan, 1990

Reiki: The Hawayo Takata's Story by H. Haberly, 1990

Living Reiki: Takata's Teachings, F. Brown, 1992

Reiki Fire by Frank Arjava Petter, 1997

Sacred Flames Reiki by Allison Dahlhaus, 2002

PRISMology by Adrien Amadeo, 2002

The Reiki Center of Venice

        The Reiki Center of Venice came into existence to help empower people to heal themselves, their families, and their communities. By sharing this light with others, we in turn are also healed. The Reiki Center of Venice offers many modalities, methods and techniques to help bring this dream of sharing and spreading the light to others.

        The Reiki Center of Venice offers Certifications for classes taken both on site and for distant learning. Below is a list of classes that are currently being taught through the Center. For more information on these and other classes that the Center offers, please visit their website at: www.Reiki.Fws1.com or drop them an email at: RevReikiND@cs.com

Traditional Usui Reiki

Tibetan Reiki

Imara Reiki

Karuna Reiki

Raku Kei Reiki

Karuna Ki

MatriVihara Reiki

Sacred Flames Reiki

Tera Mai Reiki

Sekhem-Seichim-Reiki

Golden Reiki

Kundalini Reiki

Mahatma Reiki

Ascension Reiki

Enhanced Reiki Training

Violet Flame Reiki

Shamballa Multi-Dimensional Healing Reiki

The Reiki Center of Venice also offers courses and certifications in other energy systems of healing. Below is a current list, as of this printing, of classes and courses that are either taught on-site or by correspondence.

Isis Seichem

Ra-Sheeba

Chios

Golden Triangle

Lemurian Facilitator

Basic Aromatherapy

Holistic Aromatherapy

Homeopathy

Bach Flower

Nutrition & Chemistry

Acupressure

Massage & Bodywork

Holistic Practices for Health & Fitness

Herbology

Reflexology

Business

Anatomy

Qigong

Tai Chi for Arthritis

Chakra Energy Worker

Ama Deus

Akashic Records

Tuning Fork Therapy

Templar Certification

The Reiki Center of Venice also offers some of its courses for continuing education credits and contact hours. This list will change in the future, so please contact the Center to see what has been added or deleted. If you have a large group of interested students who would like to take some of Francine's classes, contact Francine at: RevReikiND@cs.com for information on Francine's schedule to travel to your area. As of this printing, the Reiki Center of Venice is a continuing' education provider for the following organizations:

NATABOC

National Athletic Trainers Association Board of Certification

NCBTMB

National Certification Board of Therapeutic Massage and Bodywork

This includes courses in:

Aromatherapy for Massage Therapists

Marketing Strategies for Massage Therapists

Chios Energy Field Healing

Tuning Fork Therapy

Chakra Movements

Makko Ho

Usui Reiki

Qigong

Xanu

DoIn

(Plus others)

Francine Milford, the owner of the Reiki Center of Venice, is also a Certified and Licensed Fitness Specialist. She is available to teach for both large groups of people, as well as, one on one. If you would like Francine to visit your group, contact her at: RevReikiND@cs.com. Francine also offers the following exercise classes:

Personal Training

Weight Training

Step Aerobics

Water Aerobics

Floor Aerobics

Hi-Lo Aerobics

Low Impact Aerobics

Cross-Training

Boot Camp

Cycling

Senior Aerobics

Basic Yoga

Trim and Tone

Makko Ho

Qigong

DoIn

Tai Chi for Arthritis

Stretching

Basics of Belly Dancing

Chakra Movement

Kick Boxing

Besides the entire courses listed, the Reiki Center of Venice also offers one day workshops and fun classes such as:

Acupressure Face Lift

Path of the Feather

Walk the Labyrinth

Meet your Guides

Empowerment through Reiki

Women's Sacred Circles

Reiki Circles

Darkroom Meditation

Meditations

Angel Circles

Angel crafts

How to See an Aura

Chakra Balancing

Chakra Cleansing

Energy Work

Mudras

How to Heal your House

Basics of Belly Dancing

Walk the Labyrinth

Chakra Movement

Sacred Woman Circles

Reiki Shares and Circles

The Medicine Wheel

Angelic Circles

Craft projects

(Plus additional classes…)

Reiki Glossary

A

Acute - Relates to an illness or disease that although severe, it has a short duration.

Angel wings – This technique is generally used at the end of a Reiki healing session that both signifies the end of the session, as well as, the closing of the chakras and smoothing out of the aura.

Antahkarana Symbol - This symbol is a cube shape with three numbers 7's on its face surface. Considered Tibetan in origin, it is used on all areas of healing.

Attunement - Attunements are a process, or system, by which the Reiki Master places the Reiki Symbols into the students' body. The student will also be able to access the Reiki energy after the attunement on their own. The attunement helps to facilitate the connection of the practitioner to the Reiki source.

Aura - A pattern of life force energy that surrounds all living things. There are several layers energy patterns within the aura.

B

Beaming - A distant healing technique to use when person, place, etc. is within sight. Used for burn victims, persons in oxygen tents, contagious people, etc.

Byosen (also called Scanning) - Process where the Reiki practitioners move their hands over the body of a client to determine any areas in need of treatment.

C

Chakra - Energy vortices or "wheels" of energy. It is Indo-Tibetan in origin. Body contains the Seven Major Chakras and various minor Chakras.

Chiryo - One of the three pillars of Reiki. The word means "treatment". Practitioners' place dominant hand over clients head and asks for guidance.

Cho-Ku-Rei - It is also called the "Power Symbol", or the "Focus Symbol". It means "God is here." And "Put the Power here." Use this symbol when you need to increase the flow of Reiki energy being received by the client.

Chronic - An illness that is long in duration (more than one year).

Cleansing - A 21-day suggested process where the body will remove toxins and realigns its energy field. Toxins are in the form of physical as well as emotional and physiological toxins. This will help to "clear" the practitioner's energy system to accept the Reiki energy.

Cocoon – This technique is the wrapping of the client into an imagined cocoon which is then filled with Reiki energy. This cocoon signifies the end of the Reiki healing session and the closing of the chakras.

D

Dai-Ko-Mio/Dai-Ko-Myo – This is the Usui Master Symbol. It is the symbol for the ultimate source of Love and Harmony. It also means, "The Great Shining Light."

Distant Healing - (Hon-Sha-Ze-Sho-Nen) – This is the method of sending Reiki energy over large distances. Healing can be sent across state line, over continents, etc.

Dumo - Also known as the Tibetan Master Symbol. This symbol is also referred to as the Tibetan Dai Ko Mio. It is said to unify the body with the mind. It is said to work in conjunction with fire in the base Chakra by igniting the Kundalini Energy. It would then pull the negative energy and disease out from the body and the mind.

E

Empowerments – The process of teacher to student helping them to use energy. In Reiki, the Reiju technique is an empowerment given by Usui to his students.

Energy - The vigor, force and power of doing mechanical work.

F

Fire Serpent – This is the Tibetan symbol representing the "Sleeping Serpent" coiling at the base of the spine. It is used in an attunement with a horizontal line over the top of the crown. It then snakes down the spine and spirals clockwise at the base of the spine. It grounds the energy into the feet and tailbone. You can then reverse the spiral by moving counter-clockwise starting at the base of the spine, snaking up the spine and ending with the horizontal line over the crown Chakra. This will move the energy up the four upper Chakras and stopping at the crown Chakra. The Fire Serpent symbol may be used to open all the Chakras in a healing session or meditation to achieve more balance and receptivity.

G

Gassho – It is one of the three pillars of Reiki. This word means, "Two hands coming together". This symbol can be used as a meditation to increase the Reiki energy.

Gyoshi Ho - A method of Healing with the Eyes. For this you will stare at the area you wish to send healing energy to and then allow that energy to come through your eyes to that area.

H

Hand Positions - These are the specific hand positions that are used in the Reiki healing session. Every school teaches a set of basic hand positions. Numbers may range from 5 to 55. Every school is different. Every master is different.

Hatsurei Ho - A meditation and breathing technique used by dr. Usui that empowers the practitioner by increasing and enhancing their Reiki channel and their connection to the Reiki source. It may help the Reiki practitioner to grow spiritually. It includes a self cleansing ritual as well as two different meditation practices.

Hayashi (Chujiro Hayashi, Dr. Hayashi) - Made a Reiki Master in 1925 by Dr. Usui. He was a retired Japanese Navy Officer. He opened a Reiki Clinic where he taught 12 standard hand positions for healing. He is also the one who taught the Reiki system to Hawayo Takata.

Healing Crisis - A healing crisis occurs when a person experiences a "release" of emotional or physical elements.

Heso Chiryo - The Navel Technique. A self-treatment technique used to calm and relax the body.

Hui-Yin Point - Located at the base of the body, it is contracted during the Microcosmic Orbit   Breath work in Qigong and contracted in the Fire/Violet Breath.

Hon Sha Ze Sho Nen - The "Distant Healing" symbol. It means, "No past, no present, no future". Use to send Reiki energy over long distances, back in time, to the present, and into the future to some event, body area, trauma, etc.

I

Intent - The most powerful tool in the Reiki system. It is the key to using the Reiki energy in healing sessions and in giving attunements.

J

Jaki Kiri Joka ho - Method used to purify and harmonize inanimate objects.

Johrei - A religion developed by Mokichi Okada, a student of Mikao Usui. It uses the White Light (Johrei) symbol as part of its practices and attunements.

Joshin Kokyu-Ho - A Breathing Exercise to help strengthen the Reiki Energy.

K

Karuna Ki - A Compassionate Heart Energy and Healing system developed by Vinny Amador sharing common symbols with Karuna Reiki and Tera Mai Reiki plus adding Mudras,   meditations and other techniques.

Karuna Reiki - A system founded by William Rand using Tera Mai Reiki and Seichem. The system is controlled and regulated through the International Center for Reiki Studies in Michigan, USA

Ken Yoku Technique -A Dry Bathing Method used to disconnect yourself from unwanted thoughts, your client's energy, etc.

Ki KO - Also called (Qi Gong). It is a Japanese Traditional Chi Kung.

KoKi-Ho – It means, "Healing with your Breath". It is called a "blowing" technique that is used in Reiki.

L

Levels in Reiki - Generally speaking, there are three levels of training in the Usui Reiki System.

M

Master Symbol - Also known as the Dai-Ko-Mio. It is the symbol that is also called the "Great Shining Light".

Meditation – Method to bring about a heightened state of consciousness. In Reiki, the Hatsurei Ho is used to achieve a meditative state.

Mental Emotional Symbol - Also known as Sei Hei Ki.

Mikao Usui - Developer of the Reiki System for Natural Healing. He was born in the village called Yago on August 15th, 1865.

N

Nin Giz Zida - Also called the "Fire Serpent"

O

Oku-den - The Second Teaching in the Reiki Ryoho in Japan.

P

Power Symbol - Also called the Cho Ku Rei.

R

Raku - The lightening shaped symbol that is used in the attunement process. It is said to separate the energies of the master and the student.

Reiho - It refers to the practices and the systems used in Usui Reiki Ryoho Gakkai

Reiki - Pronounced (ray-key). It is a system of hands on healing developed in the early 1900s by Mikao Usui in Japan. Translates into "Universal Light Force Energy"

Reiju - An original empowerment used by Mikao Usui to pass on the Reiki energy. Reiju are the Attunements that are now being used in all western reiki systems.

Reiki Alliance - An organization formed by Mrs. Takata's granddaughter, Mrs. Phyllis Furumoto. It practices the Hayashi-Takata lineage.

Reiki Circle – Reiki circle, or share, as it is sometimes called. It is a Group of practitioners who get together to share Reiki energy.

Reiki Crystal Grid – This is a technique that uses Reiki and requires the use of crystals. A grid is created using crystals to enhance the energy and Reiki is infused into the grid. This is generally taught in the later Reiki levels.

Reiki Guides - Some believe that every student who receives the Reiki attunements also receives a Reiki Guide to help them with their practice.

Reiki Master - A Reiki practitioner who has successfully completed all levels of Reiki training and is now teaching the Reiki system to others.

Reiki Principles - A series of five sayings written by the Meiji Emperor and used by the Usui in Reiki Ryoho. They are designed to help empower the students and bring about an awakened mental and spiritual state.

Reiki Stacks - A technique of sending distant Reiki energy. Where you add several names on a list and send Reiki to them. A stack is also a number of practitioners who can lay their hands on top of each other in a healing session. One may also put their hands on the back of another practitioner to help increase the energy sent.

S

Scanning - A method of moving your hands over a client's body to detect any areas in need of treatment. Areas of heat, cold, pulsating, etc. can be felt.

Sei-Hei-Ki – This is also called the Mental/Emotional Symbol. This symbol is also known as the "Harmony Symbol". Used to help heal on the mental and emotional levels in the body

Shoden - The First teachings in the Reiki Ryoho Gakkai.

Shinpi den – It is the Fourth teaching, or "Mystery Teachings" in the Usui Reiki Ryoho.

T

Takata - (Mrs. Hawayo Takata) – She was a student of Chujiro Hayashi. She was the first Reiki Master to be allowed to teach Reiki in the western world.

Tibetan Reiki – This is the school of Reiki training which teaches additional levels and symbols.

Tibetan Master Symbol - Also known as "Dumo".

Traditional Japanese Reiki – This is a school of Reiki that does not include the Takata lineage. It was developed by Dave King in Canada.

U

Usui Shiki Ryoho - Refers to the Reiki of the Hayashi lineage and the Hayashi-Takata lineage. It is the most common Reiki practiced in the western world.

Usui Reiki Hikkei - This is the Usui Reiki Handbook that Mikao Usui gave to his students. It contained four parts, the "Teachings of Usui Reiki Ryoho", "Explanation of Instruction for the Public", "Method of Healing Guide", and the "Poems of the Meiji Emperor".

Usui Reiki Ryoho - The practice of Reiki as Usui practiced it and is still practiced in Japan today. Reiju empowerments are used instead of Attunements.

Usui/Tibetan Reiki - School of Reiki that has four levels. This school uses crystals, guides, healing attunements and various "Tibetan" symbols.

V

Vajra Reiki - A system of Reiki that uses some of the Tibetan Material as well as the White Light (Johre) symbol.

Violet Breath - Also known as the "Breath of the Fire Dragon". Used in healing and in the attunement process.

About the Author

Francine Milford
Reiki Center of Venice
P.O. Box 554
Venice, Fl. 34293

Francine Milford is a Holistic Practitioner and owner of the Reiki Center of Venice. She is an inspirational teacher and continuing education provider for many National Certifying Boards. She spends most of her time on the computer updating her courses and manuals, as well as, working on some new therapies and techniques.

Francine Milford has attained Reiki Mastership through several lineages and brings her combined knowledge of energy work into her classes. Having experience in the Fitness Industry as a Personal Trainer and Aerobic Instructor, she has created a series of workshops and classes that combine the Body, the Mind and the Spirit.

Francine offers a warm can do attitude in relating her own story of healing from debilitating and blinding migraines and constant panic attacks. Through combining breathing techniques, relaxation techniques, diet and exercise, along with Reiki, Francine has been symptom free for over 5 years. It was during this time that Francine discovered her severe reactions to chemical drugs that were first prescribed to her by conventional doctors. "I didn't want to live like a zombie, dependent on pills. I wanted my health back and I began to search for the answers." Her search leads her to study Herbology, Aromatherapy, Acupressure, Reflexology, and more. After several years of study and practicing various methods and techniques, Reiki was the icing on the cake. Francine now teaches courses in Alternative Therapies both on site and by correspondence courses. Students can work at their own pace starting with one lesson at a time.

"I believe in self empowering my students." Francine is hardly finished in her learning of additional systems of healing. "With every new system of healing, there is something I can take away from it and incorporate into my own practice. Learning never ends and I am enjoying the journey." You can view some of Francine's courses and class schedules on her websites at:

www.Reiki.Fws1.com

www.ReikiCenter.50megs.com

www.ReikiMinistry.Faithweb.com

My Usui Lineage
(1)

Dr. Mikao Usui

Dr. Hayashi

Mrs. Takata

Phyllis Furumoto

Claudia Hoffman

Mary Shaw

Christine Henderson

Bruce Way

Ariane McMinn

Allison Dahlhaus

Francine Milford

My Usui Lineage
(2)

Mikao Usui

Chjiro Hayashi

Hawayo Takata

Phyllis Furumoto

Evelyne Helbling

Miranda & Peter Gilgen

Ageh & Unmesha Popad

Frank Arjava Petter

Henry Becker

Francine Milford

My Usui Lineage
(3)

Mikao Usui

Chjiro Hayashi

Hawayo Takata

Phyllis Furumoto

Evelyne Helbling

Miranda & Peter Gilgen

Ageh & Unmesha Popad

William Rand

Henry Becker

Francine Milford

My Usui Lineage
(4)

Mikao Usui

Chujiro Hayashi

Hawayo Takata

Phyllis Lei Furumoto

Carroll Ann Farmer

Leah Smith

William Rand

Rev. Joseph Sparti

Rev. Arla Ruggless

Dr. Aurelian Curin

Francine Milford

My Usui Lineage
(5)

Mikao Usui

Chujiro Hayashi

Hawayo Takata

Phyllis Lei Furumoto

Carroll Ann Farmer

Leah Smith

William Rand

Light and Adonea

Zach Keyer

Dr. Aurelian Curin

Francine Milford

My Usui Lineage
(6)

Mikao Usui

Chujiro Hayashi

Hawayo Takata

Phyllis Lei Furumoto

Carroll Ann Farmer

Leah Smith

William Rand

Rev. Joseph Sparti

Dr. Aurelian Curin

Francine Milford

The Attunement Process

What is an Attunement?

An attunement is given to every Reiki student by the Reiki master. This attunement is a process of opening the student's energy centers to connect to and accept the flow of Reiki energy into their body. Depending on which lineage you are learning from, there can be anywhere from one to four separate attunements done in the Reiki level one training. Following the study of Level One training, each student is expected to go home and practice the hand positions for healing themselves that they were taught in class. They should practice these hand positions every night for at least 21 nights (longer if they feel more is needed). They should also do these hand positions before continuing on their education and study with Reiki 2.

The cleansing process will help to strengthen the student by opening any blockages they may have in their energy systems. Some students cry a lot, some laugh a lot, and some just plain go to sleep. We are all on a different leg of our journey, so depending on where you are right now in your spiritual walk will depend what type of cleansing your body will go through. The results are well worth the effort.

Open yourself up to spirit and new possibilities. Let the old wash away from you, it doesn't serve your highest self anymore. Dare to venture out of your box and explore new pathways to healing. Reiki was the single most precious gift given to me for self healing. It has been a great privilege to be able to share this with the world.

And now, as my gift to you, I want to offer you a free Reiki Level One attunement. For anyone who has purchased this book and has read it and felt a connection to it and my words, I offer you this free gift of a Reiki Level One attunement. Drop me an email when you are ready to receive your attunement and we shall set up a day and time for me to send you (long distance) a Reiki level one attunement. This offer is only for a long distant attunement. You can reach me at my email address at (RevReikiND@cs.com). Please, no phone calls or letters that I have to answer or return. I apologize, but I do not have the time or desire to respond to other forms of communication and will not perform an attunement over the phone. You must respect my time and my family time.

There are no strings attached. I only ask that you use this gift of Reiki to heal yourself, your family, and all those around you. Be another ripple in the water and spread the loving and healing energy of Reiki.

When you have received your attunement through me via long distance, you can begin using your Reiki energy on yourself and those around you. It is with loving gratitude that I share this with you and world. The attunement is free, the certificate is not. If you would like to receive a Certificate to commemorate your Reiki 1 attunement, an order form is available for your use on the next page. Certificate is suitable for framing.

How to Prepare for the Attunement

The attunement is a sacred vehicle by which the student receives the ability to access the healing energy of Reiki. This is not to be taken lightly. It is expected that the student will prepare themselves both physically, mentally, emotionally, and spiritually for this event. To prepare physically, the student should eat a very light meal or no meal at all one hour before the attunement time. The student should also perform some type of cleansing and purification ritual before the attunement. A few ideas for those of you who are new to cleansing and purifications rituals would be some of the following:

Take a shower and imagine your entire body and aura being cleansed of impurities.

Smudging

Smudging is the burning of white sage. To perform this ceremony you will need to purchase a twig of white sage and a container to hold the ashes in. You will light the sage and then blow the fire out. What you will have left is smoke. It is this smoke that you will use for the smudging process. You will take this smoke and swirl it all around you. Native Americans use smudging as a way of cleansing and purification. You can also take this smoke to the corners of the room that you are going to be sitting in to receive your attunement.

Meditation

You should sit quietly before the appointed attunement time and calm and center yourself. Free your mind of all the days' obligations and relax. There are some excellent meditation tapes on the market if you need to practice before the attunement. Those who are already adept in the art of meditation may choose to play a calming tape in the background. Music of birds singing, water running, and wind blowing are some examples of calming tapes that are available for purchase in almost every store today.

Other Considerations

Other considerations would be for you to unplug your phones, answering machines, turn off the computer, etc. This should be a quiet and undisturbed time for you. You may also choose to sit on the floor in a lotus position, sit on a chair with your feet firmly on the ground, or even lay on a bed or a massage table. The choice is up to you. Choose a position that is both comfortable and convenient for you. You should be able to stay this position for at least 20 minutes until the attunement process is complete.

Mentally, try to prepare yourself with your expectations. I suggest you have no expectations going into the attunement process. Every student is different and every attunement is different. You may feel nothing at all. You may feel vibrations, see colors, feel the hair on your arms stand up, and see visions. All things are possible. If you go into the attunement process without expectations, the attunement will run much more smoothly and easily.

Emotionally, try to put your own ego behind you. Do not expect to have a cure for your disease or a complete healing because you are being attuned. This could happen, but it rarely does. In your mind prepare yourself for the fact that you will soon be on a journey of self discovery. It may be a long, long process. Accept that.

Now, how you can prepare yourself spiritually for the Reiki attunement. The student must realize that the healing power of Reiki is both an internal as well as external form of healing energy. Yes, you find remarkable results using Reiki on injuries of the body. More importantly, you will begin to notice remarkable results on injuries of the body that you can't see. Injuries such loneliness, depression, anger, hopelessness and so much more may be healed using Reiki healing energy. There are no guarantees or promises made with the use of Reiki. For Reiki practitioners know this, using Reiki can heal on all levels of the human condition. This includes the physical, the mental, the emotional, and the spiritual. This is a journey of self discovery and empowerment.

To receive your own Official Certificate suitable for framing and signed by the Author,

Send $20.00 in check or money order to:

Reiki Center of Venice

P.O. Box 554

Venice, Fl. 34284-0554

Please allow 4-6 weeks for delivery of your certificate.

If you live outside of the Continental United States, please add an additional $10.00 for postage and handling expenses. ($30.00 total)

Please print your name as it is to appear on your certificate on the line below:

_____

Address to send Certificate:

Name: _____

Address: _____

City: _____

State: _____

Zip Code: _____

Email Address: _____

Are you a Reiki Master who would like to use this manual in your own Reiki classes? If so, please contact me for information on quality discounts on this manual.

Contact Francine Milford at: RevReikiND@cs.com

"May Light and Love be with you always"

Francine

Printed in the United Kingdom
by Lightning Source UK Ltd.
125695UK00002B/105/A